Partners

Partners

Veronica Geng

1817

HARPER & ROW, PUBLISHERS, New York

Cambridge, Philadelphia, San Francisco, London

Mexico City, São Paulo, Sydney

Grateful acknowledgments to Frederick Barthelme for the drawings of failed neckties on p. 64; and to Carlos Clarens for photo research. Photos on pp. 25–34 from Photothèque and Jerry Ohlinger's Movie Material Store, Inc.

"The Revised Dictionary of Slang and Uncontrollable English" was published in somewhat different form under the title "Prime Time Terms" in *The Eighties: A Look Back,* edited by Tony Hendra, Christopher Cerf, and Peter Elbling (Workman Publishing Company, Inc., New York). Copyright © 1979 United Multinationals, Inc.

"Lulu in Washington" originally appeared in *American Film;* "Pac Hits Fan" and "Pepys's Secret Diaries!" in *The New Republic;* "James at an Awkward Age" in *The New York Review of Books;* "Curb Carter Policy Discord Effort Threat" in *Not The New York Times;* and "Ten Movies That Take Women Seriously" in *Soho News.* The following pieces originally appeared, in slightly different form, in *The New Yorker:* "Report from Your Congressman," "My Mao," "The Sixth Man," "Partners," "Buon Giorno, Big Shot," "A Man Called José," "Petticoat Power," "What Makes Them Tick," "More Mathematical Diversions," "Teaching Poetry Writing to Singles," "The Stylish New York Couples," "Masterpiece Tearjerker," "Serenade," "Kemp, Dent in Reagan Plans," "Record Review," "Indecent Indemnity," "Now at West Egg," "Supreme Court Roundup," and "Lobster Night."

FIRST EDITION

Designer: C. Linda Dingler

Library of Congress Cataloging in Publication Data

Geng, Veronica.
    Partners.

    I. Title.
PN6162.G374 1984   818'.5407   83-48812
ISBN 0-06-015295-8

---

84 85 86 87 88 10 9 8 7 6 5 4 3 2 1

To my brother, Steve

Contents

PARTNERS

Report from Your Congressman   3
Lulu in Washington   9
My Mao   17
Ten Movies That Take Women Seriously   24
The Sixth Man   35
Partners   39

WHAT MAKES THEM TICK

Buon Giorno, Big Shot   45
A Man Called José   48
Petticoat Power   52
What Makes Them Tick   59
More Mathematical Diversions   61
James at an Awkward Age   67
Teaching Poetry Writing to Singles   72
The Stylish New York Couples   78
Masterpiece Tearjerker   82

COMING APART AT THE SEMES

Serenade   91
Curb Carter Policy Discord Effort Threat   102
Kemp, Dent in Reagan Plans   104
The Reagan History of the United States   108
Pac Hits Fan   114
The Sacred Front   117
The Revised Dictionary of Slang and
        Uncontrollable English   136
Coming Apart at the Semes   141

SUPREME COURT ROUNDUP

Record Review   151
Indecent Indemnity   156
Now at West Egg   167
Supreme Court Roundup   169
Lobster Night   173
Pepys's Secret Diaries!   182

Partners

Report from
Your Congressman

DEAR CONSTITUENT:

As the new year is evidently under way, I am completing a nearly striving-packed decade as your full-time Representative in Washington, D.C. I want you to know how firmly I have urged you to support me, and how deeply I appreciate the authority you have vested in me to exceed my authority. As your Representative, I played a cameo role in last year's Legislative Session, during which a substantial number of new laws were enacted under or near my sponsorship or with my vigorous opposition. Here are some highlights:

- toughened penalties against juveniles who escape from middle-income housing
- outlawed lethal incentives
- streamlined "Saturday Night Special" judicial-selection procedures
- mandated pending evaluation
- simulated energy

As your full-time Representative, I have been fully concerned with expanding my priority concerns. Here are some focal points:

- teen-age grand juries
- turnstile preservation
- costly and inefficient urban coalitions
- "head shops" at consulates and missions to U.N.
- transportation bootlegging
- subhuman conditions in Off-Track Betting parlors
- no-fault gang warfare
- gene-splicing discounts for senior citizens
- fiasco control
- clearinghouse habitability
- ombudsman repatriation

UGLY PROBLEM

Until recent years, the ugly problem of absentee housing has been virtually ignored. Now a full-page report prepared by my staff shows that "ugly problem" is merely one of those sociological euphemisms.

My full-time family has been a source of great strength to me during my years in the House. L. to r.: My family.

TRIGGER LEVELS OF UNEMPLOYMENT: ALBATROSS OR SAFETY NET?

Amid some unemployment, from men to women, such problems are offset by a situation that is serious but not critical, yet nonetheless stops short of complete success. Not only have unemployment figures belied employment but also employment has not prevented unemployment. It is imperative that we note that the battle seems to go on without end. Recent events would indicate that it does.

On December 3rd, I telephoned the Bureau des Élections in Paris to ask whether the French government intended to hold full, free, and democratic elections in the near future, as promised. Seated next to me are full-time executives of the Bell Telephone Company, which placed the long-distance call.

A SENSATIONAL PLACE

Individual efforts directed against the specter of federal takeover of private businesses *can* succeed. On December 15th, district resident John Occupant tasted victory when John's Restaurant opened to the public after a series of meetings with accountants and wholesalers from the area. On a full-time study of the location, I saw the fine comments which informed and articulate local spokespersons inscribed on photographs decorating the walls of this community project:

- Dear Johnny, You've been fabulous. Thank you for your hospitality.
- John's has the BEST Italian food!
- To Johnny, with love and appreciation.
- To John, Mucho aloha!
- John: And to think I weighed 90 pounds when I met you!
- To John: What a fun dinner. Kindest regards always.

TV APPEARANCE

On Sunday, December 23rd, I gave an interview on the NBC program *NewsNewsNews*. Following is a brief excerpt from the transcript ("A" is the voice of your Congressman):

Q: A lot of people are against it.

A: Well, I must say, Bill, particularly as a Congressman, people can be for or against a lot of things—

Q: Are you for or are you saying you're against it?

A: —and some of their reasons, you know, some of them have some merit.

Q: Now, what is your position?

A: Yeah, I mean, not only that but I want to emphasize repeatedly, Bill, that we frankly just don't have the answer, though, to that, as yet. And we wouldn't in Red China be able to have this full, free, and open discussion, by the way. And Bill, I want to congratulate you for asking me. The questions have been just brilliant.

Q: Well, it is certainly no secret that you have been a guest in our studio today.

EFFORT PAYS OFF

I am pleased to announce that U.S. Customs officials at J.F.K. International Airport recently confiscated a quantity of Genoese bobbin lace concealed between the pages of a copy of *Childe Harold's Pilgrimage,* by George Gordon, Lord Byron.

QUESTIONNAIRE

This month's question relates to rumor dispelment. Which of the following strategies would you support?
- ☐ fire into the air
- ☐ fire over the heads of the crowd
- ☐ fire in the neighborhood of the core group
- ☐ bomb only those using legibly written or typed provocative remarks
- ☐ pump five bullets into the rumor itself

LATIN AMERICA

Earlier this month I visited the southern cone of Latin America, where I enjoyed touring the Avalanche of Smut. I also

In a spontaneous gesture, I visited my personal family in the hospital.

renewed contact with the many fine full-time Latin-American contacts I maintain through an unofficial instrumentality in corporate form. While we cannot expect to find a complete solution at the federal level, I was heartened by the response from a Chilean general. Under my questioning, he admitted, "You see, there are no guns here. We are throwing them all into the desert."

THE UPCOMING ELECTION

Whoever my opponents will be, their records as legislators and as persons who were active during the Nixon Administration will raise questions. There is already a growing and, I believe, dangerous tendency. A lack of leadership is no substitute for inaction. That's why I challenged all of my opponents *last* year—in head-to-head debate, singlehandedly.

What kinds of things worry you? Probably the same things that worry me. Hopes. Dreams. Major thrusts. The night after I first took the oath of office, nine years ago, I dreamed that someone suggested I go somewhere or buy some tickets to something. By now, I have learned how to meet tough positions head on. That's why I want full-time to continue to serve you in the House of Representatives. There is much more to be said. Please vote for me so that I can say it.

RECYCLED ON PRINTED PAPER

Lulu in Washington

And so I have remained, in cruel pursuit of truth
and excellence, an inhumane executioner of the
bogus, an abomination to all but those few people
who have overcome their aversion to truth in order
to free whatever is good in them.
—Louise Brooks, *Lulu in Hollywood*

One evening in January 1929, while I was reading a book at
supper in the expensive Park Avenue apartment of an ugly,
vulgar banker, I received an urgent cablegram from J. Edgar
Hoover, asking me to appear in a clandestine film of a sex
party among government officials. The offer I did not consider
unusual. I had never truckled to convention, having learned
early to face the fact that I would always be disgusted by a
society which had a social mentality. Nor had I any idea that
other actors submitted to the enslavement of performing, like
monkeys, with a public in mind. Due to a mere accident of
birth, which at the time I took no notice of, I was erotically
irresistible to both men and women, but false humility was a
gift I had been denied. I never knew how to suppress my scorn
for actors who, sheeplike, could awaken lust only in that
mooing, ravenous herd which must buy its sensations with
nickels obediently shelled out at the box office. The pistol of
my talent I fired straight at my own heart. And so, when the
banker cautioned me that my eagerness to abandon Broadway
and Hollywood for Mr. Hoover's private venture might be a

self-delusion, I could only reflect how little he had bothered to learn about me as I lay reading in his bedroom every night.

I had always been abnormally truthful, though it never occurred to me to be vain about it. My integrity, like my sexual beauty, came so naturally that I was quite mystified by the attention it drew if I happened to mention it. Thus it was that the banker's presumption in questioning my self-knowledge, which I specialized in, I saw through as a pathetically ill-disguised alibi for keeping me in New York as his private property to flatter his ego. I left for Washington, packing only his first editions. Having often told him he was too stupid to appreciate them, I could not be so sanctimonious as to leave them in his possession.

Half a century later, a Southern boy who came to my hotel room canvassing for Jimmy Carter was shocked when I gave him a few sense impressions of what Washington had been like between the wars. Seeing him then adjust his clothing in a nervous, Puritanical way, and unwilling to be taken for one of those women who like to seduce young men with lying promises of pleasure, I laid out some facts in a cold, joyless manner. At the Adlon-on-the-Potomac, the hotel where I stayed in Washington in 1929, the coffeeshop was headquarters for the local pimps, readily identifiable by their loose-leaf "briefing books." Tramps dabbled their aching feet in the big Reflecting Pool, while just across the gardens Constitution Hall offered, for a price, a choice of buxom or flat-chested Daughters of the American Revolution. Round and round the Ellipse strolled lobbyists whose black leather shoes advertised sadomasochism. Farther east, off Capitol Hill, Supreme Court clerks who to my knowledge had never opened a book held sixteenth-century-death-cult orgies at the Folger Shakespeare Library. Literally a slave market was the so-called Senate, where one day from the Visitors' Gallery I saw a peroxide-blond lesbian German tourist auctioned off, by a Senator from California, to a constituent from Paramount Pictures. (I was the only person not startled with disbelief when I realized, years later, that the buyer had been Paramount's young director Josef von Sternberg. His "discovery" of the woman, in 1930, in Germany, as "Marlene Dietrich," was the fraud I had known must be at the bottom of her curious stardom, which was so baffling.)

These hypocrites, along with certain respectable citizens of the type who hated me and spent their weekends in the National Gallery pretending to ogle the culturally acceptable repression of second-rate quattrocento madonnas, were quite predictably outraged when a leak to the press, which I never had anything to do with, confronted *tout* Washington with an all too accurate image of itself in the title of our film, *D.C. Sex Party.*

The tragedy of a girl too unflinchingly honest to aspire to anything more than passive amorality: our theme was no less than that of Sophocles' *Antigone* and Ziegfeld's *Weimar Golddiggers of 1922.* Only the dull brains of carrion-mongering "columnists," who, being illiterate, disliked me, could have conceived the rumor that *D.C. Sex Party* was a crude, hasty improvisation designed merely to give J. Edgar Hoover embarrassing footage with which to blackmail his enemies in the Administration. On the contrary, the Director, as Hoover was called by the entire cast and crew, had for years contemplated the material of *D.C. Sex Party,* turning over and over in his mind its disturbing scenes of a woman's erotic degradation at the hands of influential men until each image burned with an unbearable clarity that sought discharge on film.

The great paradox of the Director's genius was that having so little worldly experience, he had acquired by compensation an uncanny power for obsessive focus on some humbly observed fact. His method was to force the fact's banal sterility into cruel bloom, releasing the clean aroma of the awful truth. This I learned the very first day of shooting, when the lesbian character called Dolly Madison was supposed to pursue me, in the "cabinet" scene, through a *Caligari*-like maze of vertiginously angled and teetering FBI fingerprint files. Unaware then that the Director had not married, I took one look at the foul, clumsy harridan cast as Dolly and at once concluded that she was his wife. After all, this sort of nepotism was universal practice in Hollywood, and why else would he have chosen her when he could have used Garbo, Dietrich, Lillian Gish, or any of the other butch types who were by that time desperate for work, their inexplicable popularity having been mercilessly sabotaged by the studios?

Just before the first take, the Director led me aside and whispered shyly, "Look, Loo-loo, just do whatever it is they say you—you know—do." I was astonished. Hollywood directors gave an actor reactions to fake and floor marks to hit, as if from a printed list; preened themselves on artistic ideals which remained inscrutable; and stole the shirt off one's back. I called them the Chinese Laundrymen. So suddenly awarded my freedom by the Director, I instinctively drew on the full energy of my natural indifference, and unerringly played the whole "pursuit" slumped against a cabinet labeled "D—Dillinger."

But the Director I had underestimated. Dolly, taken aback at my failure to put up any resistance, which in a single stroke had undercut her most effective scene, glanced briefly past me to make sure the camera was still rolling (it was) and then throttled me. Writhing frantically under those huge, hairy hands, I met "her" gaze and realized I was looking into the eyes of Secretary of State Henry Stimson in a dress. Whereupon I, in a rage at having been duped—I, who asked, and gave, nothing but the truth!—stripped his fingers from my throat and violently forced them again and again onto a nearby ink pad and fingerprint form. And so it was that the Director not only furthered his grand design but liberated in me a dynamism I had always secretly known I possessed.

Stimson, who ever after detested me, quit the picture in a huff, so I suggested that the Director replace him with Humphrey Bogart, who at the time happened to be working just a few blocks away as a hustler at Union Station. Despite Humphrey's loathing for me, I was the first to claim that he had once been the greatest dramatic actor of an otherwise pitiful bunch. His limits, though, were keenly exposed when he appeared with someone like Bojangles Robinson or Fred Astaire, who easily blew him off the screen with their almost musical quality. Sadly, Humphrey's work had turned to rubbish after I lost interest in him. However, certain that he had retained his talent for cross-dressing, I longed to see him in marabou-trimmed mules in the scene where Dolly was to discover me with my head in the lap of the Congressional page. Decades later, D. W. Griffith disagreed with me, saying that alongside me Bogart "would have looked too phony," and I had to concede that audiences always felt he was in some sense playing a part. Anyway, the economy-minded Director omitted the remainder of Dolly's role and went on to shoot the "Cabinet" sequence, in which, slashed with jagged shadows prefiguring my murder by the head of the General Accounting Office, I permitted my flesh to receive the fingerprints of Commerce, Labor, Navy, War, and Treasury.

Off the set, the Director stringently curtailed my behavior. That I was told to keep early hours, however, did not dissuade me from slipping out of my room one evening. After the first hard week of work, I longed for a promenade down Pennsylvania Avenue to investigate the nightclubs around the Marine Barracks in a flimsy concoction of silk threads and sequins which had cost a friend of mine five thousand dollars. The coast was clear, but going down the hotel stairs I found my path blocked by the Director, whose sixth sense could penetrate the very walls. On the spot he gruffly telephoned the wardrobe mistress: "Get Loo-loo three of the suits." The next day, all my own beautiful dresses were taken away and replaced with white Arrow shirts, black neckties, and shapeless jackets and trousers of some cheap black cloth. In tears, I protested to the Director: "I can't go out in these! No one will know that under all these clothes I am naked."

"*You* will," he said.

Thereafter, inflamed by imaginative truth, my powers were fully at the service of the Director.

The only time I saw the Director crack a smile was the day he heard me tell Secretary of the Treasury Andrew Mellon that a lifelong habit of candor made me helpless to hide my contempt for his social-climbing affectations and Neanderthal mug. Taking me aside, the Director again turned one of my unfocused instincts to profitable purpose: "Loo-loo, have you noticed that every time you talk about your integrity, people reach for their wallets?"

The day after we wrapped the picture, of whose fate I never heard anything, the press jackals roused themselves from a sated slumber to report in lurid detail the murder of Vicki, the dear little redheaded script girl who had been the only person on the set I ever saw reading. I recalled that she had slept with the House Majority Leader during location shooting of the "Congressional junket" sequence in Atlantic City. During those few days, in February, the pounding gray fists of the ocean had seemed to me, like Vicki's puny affair, somehow chill and unloving. Her body was found, violated and dismembered, in a wooded area near Washington's Zoological Park, where only the roars and squawks of inhuman animals penetrated.

The incontrovertible fact of this real girl's unfortunate end was all that remained of *D.C. Sex Party* as far as I was concerned, and perhaps was what most needed to be remembered, proving as it did everything I had ever said. Whether the public accepted this proof I know not, but at any rate they talked of the "Vicki case" and nothing else until the stock market crashed. The reels of film, for all anyone cared, might as well have been thrust into the briefcase of some bureaucrat who, driving home from work, chucked them to the bottom of the Potomac.

The future would be more generous, which it is easy to be when at odds with the truth. But let people think whatever they want; no longer can I be bothered to carp at such tributes as this, from a recently revised encyclopedia of film:

No negative or print of *D.C. Sex Party* is believed to exist, except for several frame enlargements of fingerprints, said to be in the secret files of J. Edgar Hoover. Nor can reviews or press releases be found, perhaps because there was some vague, now long-forgotten scandal about the death of a female crew member. Yet, like the other lost works of the silent era, *D.C. Sex Party* was undoubtedly a titanic masterpiece of cinematic sublimity which we will never, never be able to see with our own eyes, remaining deprived for all time of a truly great classic and thus insuring it a permanent place in motion-picture history and criticism. According to persons who viewed the daily rushes, the film established Hoover as an artist at once enigmatic and technically peerless, with a manneristic style that juxtaposed filaments and whorls of darkness and light to create a pictorial and spatial universe in whose very falsity lay its profound mystery

and beauty. Deceptively tawdry in outline, Hoover elicited perform-
ances of such baroque stylization and intensity that their splendor
plumbed the most Jacobean surfaces of the human soul. That of
Lulu, in particular, was a triumph of artifice.

My Mao

"Kay, would you like a dog? . . . " Ike asked.
"Would I? Oh, General, having a dog would be heaven!"
"Well," he grinned, "if you want one, we'll get one."
—*Past Forgetting: My Love Affair
with Dwight D. Eisenhower*

"I don't want you to be alone," he said after a while.
"I'm used to it."
"No, I want you to have a dog."
—*A Loving Gentleman: The Love Story
of William Faulkner and Meta Carpenter*

Why this reminiscence, this public straining of noodles in the
colander of memory? The Chairman despised loose talk. Each
time we parted, he would seal my lips together with spirit gum
and whisper, "Mum for Mao." During our ten-year relationship, we quarreled only once—when I managed to dissolve the
spirit gum with nail-polish remover and told my best friend
about us, and it got back to a relative of the Chairman's in
Mongolia. For one month the Chairman kept up a punishing
silence, even though we had agreed to write each other daily
when it was not possible to be together. Finally, he cabled this
directive: "ANGRILY ATTACK THE CRIMES OF SILLY BLABBER-
MOUTHS." I knew then that I was forgiven; his love ever wore
the tailored gray uniform of instruction.

Until now, writing a book about this well-known man has
been the farthest thing from my mind—except perhaps for

writing a book about someone else. I lacked shirts with cuffs to
jot memorandums on when he left the room. I was innocent of
boudoir electronics. I failed even to record the dates of his
secret visits to this country (though I am now free to disclose
that these visits were in connection with very important official
paperwork and high-powered meetings). But how can I hide
while other women publish? Even my friends are at it. Betty
Ann is writing *Konnie!: Adenauer in Love.* Cathy and Joan are
collaborating on *Yalta Groupies.* And my Great-Aunt Harriet
has just received a six-figure advance for *"Bill" of Particulars:
An Intimate Memoir of William Dean Howells.* Continued silence on my part would only lead to speculation that Mao
alone among the greatest men of the century could not command a literate young mistress.

That this role was to be mine I could scarcely have foreseen
until I met him in 1966. He, after all, was a head of state, I a
mere spangle on the midriff of the American republic. But you
never know what will happen, and then it is not possible to
remember it until it has already happened. That is the way
things were with our first encounter. Only now can I truly see
the details of the Mayflower Hotel in Washington, with its
many halls and doors, its carpeted Grand Suite. I can feel the
static electricity generated by my cheap nylon waitress's dress,
the warmth of the silver tray on which I hoisted a selection of
pigs-in-blankets.

Chairman Mao was alone. He sat in the center of the room,
in an upholstered armchair—a man who looked as if he might
know something I didn't. He was round, placid, smooth as a
cheese. When I bent over him with the hors d'oeuvres, he said
in perfect English but with the mid-back-rounded vowels
pitched in the typical sharps and flats of Shaoshan, "Will you
have a bite to eat with me?"

"No," I said. In those days, I never said yes to anything. I
was holding out for something better.

He closed his eyes.

By means of that tiny, almost impatient gesture, he had hinted that my way of life was wrong.

I felt shamed, yet oddly exhilarated by the reproof. That night I turned down an invitation to go dancing with a suture salesman who gamely tried to date me once in a while. In some way I could not yet grasp, the Chairman had renewed my sense of possibility, and I just wanted to stay home.

One evening about six months later, there was a knock at my door. It was the Chairman, cheerful on rice wine. With his famous economy of expression, he embraced me and taught me the Ten Right Rules of Lovemaking: Reconnoiter, Recruit, Relax, Recline, Relate, Reciprocate, Rejoice, Recover, Reflect, and Retire. I was surprised by his ardor, for I knew the talk that he had been incapacitated by a back injury in the Great Leap Forward. In truth, his spine was supple as a peony stalk. The only difficulty was that it was sensitive to certain kinds of pressure. A few times he was moved to remind me, "Please, don't squeeze the Chairman."

When I awoke the next morning, he was sitting up in bed with his eyes closed. I asked him if he was thinking. "Yes," he said, without opening his eyes. I was beginning to find his demeanor a little stylized. But what right did I have to demand emotion? The Cultural Revolution had just started, and ideas of the highest type were surely forming themselves inside his skull.

He said, "I want to be sure you understand that you won't see me very often."

"That's insulting," I said. "Did you suppose I thought China was across the street?"

"It's just that you mustn't expect me to solve your problems," he said. "I already have eight hundred million failures at home, and the last thing I need is another one over here."

I asked what made him think I had problems.

He said, "You do not know how to follow Right Rule Number Three: Relax. But don't expect me to help you. Expect nothing."

I wanted to ask how I was supposed to relax with a world figure in my bed, but I was afraid he would accuse me of personality cultism.

When he left, he said, "Don't worry."

I thought about his words. They had not been completely satisfying, and an hour after he had left I wanted to hear them again. I needed more answers. Would he like me better if I had been through something—a divorce, a Long March, an evening at Le Club? Why should I exhaust myself in relaxation with someone who was certain to leave? Every night after work I studied the Little Red Book and wrote down phrases from it for further thought: "woman . . . certain contradictions . . . down on their knees . . . monsters of all kinds . . . direct experience."

My life began to feel crowded with potential meaning. One afternoon I was sitting in the park, watching a group of schoolchildren eat their lunch. Two men in stained gray clothing lay on the grass. Once in a while they moved discontentedly from a sunny spot to a shady spot, or back again. The children ran around and screamed. When they left, one of the men went over to the wire wastebasket and rifled the children's lunch bags for leftovers. Then he baited the other man in a loud voice. He kept saying, "*You* are not going downtown, Tommy. *We* are going downtown. *We* are going downtown."

Was this the "social order" that the Chairman had mentioned? It seemed unpleasant. I wondered if I should continue to hold out.

As it happened, I saw him more often than he had led me to expect. Between visits, there were letters—his accompanied by erotic maxims. These are at present in the Yale University Library, where they will remain in a sealed container until all the people who are alive now are dead. A few small examples will suggest their nature:

My broom sweeps your dust kittens.
Love manifests itself in the hop from floor to pallet.
If you want to know the texture of a flank, someone must roll over.

We always met alone, and after several years *dim sum* at my place began to seem kind of hole-in-corner. "Why don't you ever introduce me to your friends?" I asked. The Chairman made no reply, and I feared being pushy. We had no claims on each other, after all, no rules but the ones he sprang on me now and then. Suddenly he nodded with vigor and said, "Yes, yes." On his next trip he took me out to dinner with his friend Red Buttons. Years later, the Chairman would often say to me, "Remember that crazy time we had dinner with Red? In a restaurant? What an evening!"

Each time we met, I was startled by some facet of his character that the Western press had failed to report. I saw, for instance, that he disliked authority, for he joked bitterly about his own. No sooner had he stepped inside my bedroom than he would order, "Lights off!" When it was time for him to go, he would raise one arm from the bed as if hailing a taxi and cry, "Pants!" Once when I lifted his pants off the back of a chair and all the change fell out of the pockets, I said, "This happens a lot. I have a drawer full of your money that I've found on the floor."

"Keep it," he said, "and when it adds up to eighteen billion yuan, buy me a seat on the New York Stock Exchange." He laughed loudly, and then did his impersonation of a capitalist. "Bucks!" he shouted. "Gimme!" We both collapsed on the bed, weak with giggles at this private joke.

He was the only man I ever knew, this pedagogue in pajamas, who did not want power over me. In conversation, he was always testing my independence of thought. Once, I remember, he observed, "Marxism has tended to flourish in Catholic countries."

"What about China?" I said.

"Is China your idea of a Catholic country?"

"No, but, um—"

"See what I mean?" he said, laughing.

I had learned my lesson.

To divest himself of sexual power over me, he encouraged me to go dancing with other men while he was away. Then we held regular critiques of the boyfriends I had acquired. My favorite, a good-looking Tex-Mex poet named Dan Juan, provided us with rich material for instruction and drill.

"What is it you like about Dan Juan?" the Chairman asked me once.

"I'd really have to think about it," I said.

"Maybe he's not so interesting," said the Chairman.

"I see your point," I said. Then, with the rebelliousness of the politically indolent, I burst into tears.

The Chairman took my hand and brooded about my situation. I think he was afraid that helping me to enter into ordinary life—to go out with Dan Juan and then to learn why I should not be going out with him and so forth—might not be very much help at all.

Finally, he said, "I don't like to think you're alone when I'm not here."

"I'm not always alone."

"I'd like to give you a radio."

The radio never reached me, although I do not doubt that he sent it. His only other gifts we consumed together: the bottles of rice wine, which we drank, talking, knowing that while this was an individual solution, it was simple to be happy. Now other women have pointed out to me that I have nothing to show for the relationship. Adenauer gave Betty Ann a Salton Hotray. Stalin gave Cathy a set of swizzlesticks with little hammer-and-sickles on the tops. William Dean Howells gave my Great-Aunt Harriet a diamond brooch in the form of five ribbon loops terminating in diamond-set tassels, and an aquamarine-and-diamond tiara with scroll and quill-pen motifs separated by single oblong-cut stones mounted on an aquamarine-and-diamond band. That I have no such mementos means, they say, that the Chairman did not love me. I think they are being too negative.

The Chairman believed that the most revolutionary word is "yes." What he liked best was for me to kiss him while murmuring all the English synonyms for "yes" that I could think of. And I feel to this day that I can check in with him if I close my eyes and say yes, yeah, aye, uh-huh, indeed, agreed, natch, certainly, okeydoke, of course, right, reet, for sure, you got it, well and good, amen, but def, indubitably, right on, yes siree bob, sure nuff, positively, now you're talking, yep, yup, bet your sweet A, O.K., roger wilco over and out.

Ten Movies That Take Women Seriously

1. A WOMAN WHO COULD HAVE GOTTEN MARRIED IF SHE WANTED TO

A completely happy woman (Jill Clayburgh) is told by her lover (Alan Bates) that he has no choice but to shoot her so that he will feel free to marry a teen-age boy (Matt Dillon). Clayburgh goes underground in Soho, where she falls in love with seven supportive men in her Smoke Enders group (Robert De Niro, Vincent Price, R. W. Fassbinder, Al Pacino, Klaus Kinski, Bruno Bettelheim, and Bob Balaban) and builds a career as a photographer, taking pictures of a streetcorner where recently divorced women come to vomit. Totally happy, she then learns that she can't be truly liberated until the men are all offered high-paying jobs in Tahiti and she can reject their proposals of marriage. Director Steven Spielberg wrings peerlessly hair-raising action sequences from the awesome quitting-smoking technology, and takes a gently wry look at the way women tend to get all weepy.

Fahrenheit 451: *Studio security guard checks a stuntwoman's bathwater for the daredevil "nervous breakdown" scene.*

2. ANNIE GET YOUR SHOGUN

Based on a nineteenth-century Australian novel about six-teenth-century Japan, adapted for the screen by Alan Alda (star of *Mr. Dalloway*). An aggressive young girl (Marlo Thomas), blackballed from a posh Melbourne men's club, asserts her independence by sailing to Kyoto and horsewhipping a samu-rai (Toshiro Mifune) because she doesn't like the cut of his jib. She falls in love with the American consul (Alda), but when he asks her to marry him, she refuses, because she is ornery.

Zen and the Art of Motorcycle Maintenance: *Marlo Thomas, the novice director, shows a complicated "dolly" shot to the Japanese crew.*

3. TWO OR THREE THINGS I CAN'T STAND ABOUT HER

Critic Andrew Sarris enters his own Pantheon with his first film—a responsible feminist-humanist remake of Brian De Palma's *Dressed to Kill.* An attractive, likable woman (Michael Palin) is in the shower when an inspector from the Gas Company intrudes into her bathroom and (in what alert cinéastes will recognize as a quote from Sarris' own film column) calls her "a grotesquely oversexed, middle-aged bourgeois bitch." She realizes this is true and cancels her shrink appointment to stay home and preheat the oven according to his guidelines. The Gas Man continues on his search for the ideal woman—a professor of quantum physics (Diane Keaton) who is upper-class, young, and moderately sexed.

I Lost It in the Movieola: *Ritual* hommage *to Hitchcock by director Sarris (l.) was among derivative scenes censored by humanistic lawyer for Hitch's estate (r.).*

4. INTERMISSION

In Lawrence Kasdan's stylish update of *Intermezzo,* a conventional married assistant curator at the Museum of Modern Art (Mick Jagger), once a socially conscious swinger and pop artist, falls in love with his daughter's role model (Carrie Fisher) and takes her with him as backup curator when he goes on the road with the Picasso show. The story is told visually, through close-ups of Fisher's gradual co-optation as she suppresses evidence of numerous forgeries among the examples of analytical cubism. The wife (Rula Lenska) stays home and tries to get a comb through her hair, while the daughter (Jade Jagger) is run over by a car full of boisterous drug addicts in order to further disillusion the audience.

The Sacking of Troy: From the 1950s Warner Bros. remake, Intermezzo Pajama Party.

5. PORTENTIMENTO

Lillian Hellman (Mia Farrow) and Mary McCarthy (Liv Ullmann) try on hats and learn to touch-type, tutored by Dashiell
Hammett (director Woody Allen) and Edmund Wilson (Pat
McCormick), while Stalin (Jerry Stiller) collectivizes the
Ukraine. Years later, at a screening of *Islands in the Stream,*
the two women meet again and Lilly confesses that she could
have married Hammett but they never got around to it.

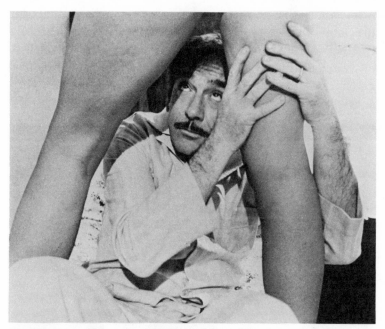

Ten Days That Shook His Confidence: *Ernest Hemingway (Jerry Stiller)
debates Lillian about the Moscow Trials.*

6. WETWORK

Karen Silkwood, a glamorous, foul-mouthed female head of programming at a TV network (Faye Dunaway), who's more ruthless than Hitler (Jerry Stiller), discovers that ratings skyrocket when the idealistic spinster weather reporter she's about to fire (Jane Fonda) cries on camera while predicting a snowstorm that will cause many people to be late for work. To induce Fonda to weep nightly, Dunaway engineers a series of plutonium-plant accidents. An AEC investigator (Jon Voight) offers Fonda the ultimate in happiness—marriage—but she turns him down to prove she's incorruptible. Under the sensitive direction of George Lucas (hired because he was mistaken for "women's director" George Cukor by the busy executive producer, George Lucas), Dunaway's and Fonda's unflattering hair-dos represent the full spectrum of liberated misery.

Mad as Hell: Silkwood's masterpiece, "The Newly Nude Game."

7. BI MOM

In this sequel to *Kramer vs. Kramer,* Joanna (Meryl Streep) has a series of love affairs with judges from Family Court (Jill Clayburgh, Liv Ullmann, and Amy Irving), while her son, Billy (now a disturbed eighteen-year-old, played by Sylvester Stallone), sues to deny her visiting rights as an unfit mother. The suit is dropped when a kindly guru (Christopher Isherwood) invites Billy to go to India with him and get his head together. Director Robert Benton deftly delineates the growing acceptance of Joanna back into the family when, at Billy's going-away party, he and his father compare penis sizes.

Penile Colony: Billy and Dad Kramer unzip for the finale.

8. THE GROOM

Can a woman's repressed rage at men manifest itself in out-
breaks of gynoculinary horror? In cult filmmaker David Cron-
enberg's latest shocker, a successful lonely career woman
(Anne Bancroft) has an affair with a married man (Ronald
Reagan), becomes pregnant, and gives birth to millions of tiny
wedding-cake grooms that threaten to annihilate the greater
Los Angeles area. Bancroft is tracked down and killed by a
lynch party, but not before she succeeds in transferring her
vengeful powers to her childhood friend (Shirley MacLaine)
when, during a hair-pulling bout, the two women discover that
they have split ends and their hair samples are switched by a
malevolent Sassoon computer.

Urban Doughboy: *John Travolta made $1 billion for achieving a mul-
tiple role.*

9. THE WOMEN'S RHEUM

Six Vassar students become unwittingly involved in a secret Department of Defense experiment to test the toxicity of over-statement. The sole survivor (Patty Duke Ellington) is be-friended by a lusty, free-spirited older wench (Elizabeth Tay-lor), who introduces her to a man strong enough to be gentle (Alan Alda). But when he is forced (by director Sidney Lumet) to present her with a choice by moving to Australia to open a medical clinic, she rejects his proposal of marriage and opts for a career in film. She moves in with a trio of supportive gay-porno stars (Dick Diver, Mao Zedong, and Francis Bacon) and makes a successful documentary, *Lenny,* proving that Leni Riefenstahl was actually a man.

Hollywood Vassarette: Professor of Modern Dance Marsha Mason (l.). Alan Alda asks, "Why is a liberated woman wearing high heels?"

10. NEXT STOP, TITLE VII

Paul Mazursky's scathing satire on the subject of sexual harassment in the office. George Segal plays an official of the Equal
Employment Opportunities Commission who is sued for harassment by his own secretary (Jill Clayburgh). In a moving
appeal to her to settle out of court by marrying him, Segal
quotes from an article by Walter Berns in the October 1980
issue of *Harper's:* "Rather than having to devote what will
surely be thousands of hours to such cases, it might be prefera-
ble to impose dress codes on female employees. . . . Men can
be aroused by what women wear and, on occasion, provoked
to do or say things they may later regret. . . . It is women, not
men, who are ultimately responsible for what might be called
the moral tone of any place where men and woman are assem-
bled, even, I think, the workplace. (Tocqueville observed this
of American women 150 years or so ago, and I think it is still
true.) In general, men will be what women want them to be.
('Do you want to know men?' asked Rousseau. 'Study women.')
An employer's 'affirmative duty to maintain a workplace free
of sexual harassment' will require that he take account of the
power women have over men."

She marries him.

Ms. *Man of the Year Trophy: Animation lends credence to Mazursky's
latest comedy of manners.*

The Sixth Man

Sir Anthony Blunt, a former curator of Queen
Elizabeth's art collection, and a renowned member
of Britain's artistic establishment, was identified by
the Government today as a long-sought "fourth
man" in the Burgess-Maclean spy case of 25 years
ago. . . . [A] supposed fifth man in the Burgess-
Maclean spy ring [has been] identified . . . only as "Basil."
—*The New York Times*, November 16, 1979

The time was the nineteen-fifties—a decade, as Frederick Jackson Turner had predicted, "with the menace of the forties at one end and the menace of the sixties at the other." For thoughtful, concerned university students in the United States, participation in the Burgess-Maclean spy ring seemed the only answer.

These troubled, idealistic young Americans were a minority, certainly, but a minority that encompassed the majority of a tiny élite. Some were heterosexuals. A number were quarterbacks, and no fewer were members of prestigious dorm councils and R.O.T.C. units. The glittering set included L.A.D. (Laddie) Dirksen, the brilliant illegitimate son of the founders of the New Criticism; N. Murray Garroway, the eminent agnostic explorer, whose father was a prominent speechwriter for Harold Stassen; H. F. Zimbalist-Lazar, effete and dissipated even as a freshman, later a noted scholar and expert on the works of Jim Bishop; and K. X. Backus—a descendant of Nathaniel Hawthorne and John Singleton Copley—who became a studio musician of enormous repute.

While these men can be linked to Burgess and Maclean only

by the kind of innuendo exemplified in the foregoing para-
graphs, a growing chain of suspicion has been forged around
them by precisely that. And now a trail of further fabrication
and distortion has led to another key figure in the plot—an
Englishman who emigrated to the United States in the early
fifties to recruit the American group. The most clever and de-
generate of them all, this long-sought "sixth man" in the case
has been identified only as "Ernest."

In an exclusive interview with this magazine, an English-
woman whom we shall call "Cecily," who knew the man as
"Ernest" in London in 1951, has come forward with evidence
that has been heard time and time again.

"Ernest seemed so very mysterious," she said. "If he was not,
he was deceiving us all in a very inexcusable manner. I hope he
was not leading a double life, pretending to be a spy and being
really loyal all the time. That would be treachery.

"It was said that at Cambridge he had called himself 'Alger-
non,' which frightened everyone so much that they attended
their lectures in groups.

"I myself was quite afraid of him. That is why I fell in love
with him. There is nothing so becoming to a young girl's com-
plexion as a love affair with someone really treasonous.

"It would hardly have been a serious affair if I had known
anything about him. Facts about most people can be endured
with equanimity. But even the slightest hint of information
about an attractive man is almost unbearable.

"One person told me with absolute authority that he had
blue eyes. Another said with equal conviction that they were
brown. I know, of course, how important it is to be inconsist-
ent if one wants to retain the opportunity for regret. But I do
feel that one has an obligation to retain one's face.

"No one could discover who his tailor was, or how much tea

he took with his lumps of sugar, or any of the other things that are always common knowledge about a traitor.

"There were all sorts of rumors about him. People said that he had entered a monastery and then, in remorse, gone out and killed a man. That he had been changed for life on account of never having learned that he had got a fatal disease. That he was from a very fine family and wished to conceal his origins. That he had been cashiered out of his regiment for refusing to slap his commanding officer. That he was passing for Bantu. That in Burma he had become addicted to Gentlemen's Relish. That he had had plastic surgery so as to make it appear that he had been mutilated in an automobile accident. That he wrote works of philosophy under an assumed name and cheap novels under his own name. That he had never kept a wife and six children in Tottenham. That he was a successful surgeon, while his colleagues had been ruined by fashionable malpractice suits. That he had a friend named Bunbury.

"All this, of course, was the gossip of unidentified sources, and consequently meant for publication.

"I liked his secretiveness. It allowed me to monopolize the conversation, and at the same time it enabled me to feel ill at ease. I dislike men who are as comfortable as an old shoe. They are so slippery.

"Sometimes I was happy just to gaze at him, the way one does at an improper picture. At other times, I found myself turning aside in embarrassment, the way one does from a really good book.

"Often I imagined that he might make love to me, tying me up and forcing me to perform vile acts. I felt sure that it would pass the time.

"He never said a single word about official secrets, so you can imagine how much he knew. And he was so attractive. In matters of espionage, sex, not politics, is the vital thing.

"I am quite sure that after he left me, he emigrated to America to recruit spies. He had a secret past; for him to have had a secret future as well would have been most unfair.

"I do think that whenever one has any secrets to impart to the Soviet Union, one should be quite candid.

"Whatever unfortunate entanglement my dear boy may have got into, I will never reproach him with it after he is imprisoned.

"And if Ernest was not the 'sixth man,' I feel sure that he was someone equally important."

Partners

The marriage of Nancy Creamer Teas, daughter of Mr. and Mrs. Russell Ruckhyde Teas of Glen Frieburg, N.Y., and Point Pedro, Sri Lanka, to John Potomac Mining, son of Mr. Potomac B. Mining of Buffet Hills, Va., and the late Mrs. Mining, took place at the First Episcopal Church of the Port Authority of New York and New Jersey.

The bride attended the Bodice School, the Earl Grey Seminary, Fence Academy, Railroad Country Day School, and the Credit School, and made her début at the Alexander Hamilton's Birthday Cotillion at Lazard Frères. She is a student in the premedical program at M.I.T. and will spend her junior year at Cartier & Cie. in Paris.

The bridegroom recently graduated from Harvard College. He spent his junior year at the Pentagon, a military concern in Washington, D.C. He will join his father on the board of directors of the Municipal Choate Assistance Corporation. His previous marriage ended in divorce.

CABINET, DELOS
NUPTIALS SET

Ellen Frances Cabinet, a self-help student at Manifest Destiny Junior College, plans to be married in August to Wengdell Delos, a sculptor, of Tampa, Fla. The engagement was announced by the parents of the future bride, Mr. and Mrs. Crowe Cabinet of New York. Mr. Cabinet is a consultant to the New York Stock Exchange.

Mr. Delos's previous marriage ended in an undisclosed settlement. His sculpture is on exhibition at the New York Stock Exchange. He received a B.F.A. degree from the Wen-El-Del Company, a real-estate-development concern with headquarters in Tampa.

MISS BURDETTE
WED TO MAN

Pews Chapel aboard the Concorde was the setting for the marriage of Bethpage Burdette to Jean-Claude LaGuardia Case, an account executive for the Junior Assemblies. Maspeth Burdette was maid of honor for her sister, who was also attended by Massapequa Burdette, Mrs. William O. Dose, and Mrs. Hodepohl Inks.

The parents of the bride, Dr. and Mrs. Morris Plains Burdette of New York, are partners in Conspicuous Conception, an art gallery and maternity-wear cartel.

The ceremony was performed by the Rev. Erasmus Tritt, a graduate of Skidmore Finishing and Divinity School and president of Our Lady of the Lake Commuter Airlines. The Rev. Tritt was attended by the flight crew. The previous marriages he has performed all ended in divorce.

DAISY LAUDERDALE
FEATURED AS BRIDE

Daisy Ciba Lauderdale of Boston was married at the Presbyterian Church and Trust to Gens Cosnotti, a professor of agribusiness at the Massachusetts State Legislature. There was a reception at the First Court of Appeals Club. The bride, an alumna of the Royal Doulton School and Loot University, is the daughter of Mr. and Mrs. Cyrus Harvester Lauderdale. Her father is retired from the family consortium. She is also a descendant of Bergdorf Goodman of the Massachusetts Bay Colony. Her previous marriage ended in pharmaceuticals.

Professor Cosnotti's previous marriage ended in a subsequent marriage. His father, the late Artaud Cosnotti, was a partner in the Vietnam War. The bridegroom is also related somehow to Mrs. Bethlehem de Steel of Newport, R.I., and Vichy, Costa Rica; Brenda Frazier, who was a senior partner with Delta, Kappa & Epsilon and later general manager of marketing for the U.S. Department of State; I. G. Farben, the former King of England; and Otto von Bismarck, vice-president of the Frigidaire Division of General Motors, now a division of The Hotchkiss School.

AFFIANCEMENT
FOR MISS CONVAIR

Archbishop and Mrs. Marquis Convair of Citibank, N.Y., have made known the engagement of their daughter, Bulova East Hampton Convair, to the Joint Chiefs of Staff of Arlington County, Va. Miss Convair is a holding company in the Bahamas.

All four grandparents of the bride-to-be were shepherds and shepherdesses.

What Makes Them Tick

Buon Giorno, Big Shot

This infamous man, this atrocious torturer, this felonious
criminal maniac, this abscess on the loin of civilization, this
V.I.P. This mystery man, this subjugator incomprehensibly
vile, whom I have killed a thousand times in my dreams.
Whom the people call Rat Excrement and Dog Scum. Whom
they call Signor X.

I heard that he never gave interviews. That he would see me
and then kill me and swallow my cassettes. For this reason I
was afraid. For this reason I was brave.

Finally he was walking toward me, across the lobby of the
Hotel Omnipotente, in Rome. God, the man is not good-
looking! The shrunken goat's-testicle of a face. The hands,
smeared as I had been told they would be with infants' blood,
each bloated finger a worm in the heart of human reasonable-
ness. Yes, I thought, he is smaller than I expected. They are
always smaller than one expects.

Let's put it this way: our interview was not charming. It was
a malady that was always going ahead to termination. Do you
know the sound of a wrecker's ball smashing an architectural
treasure of Western Europe? His voice was like that. But I
don't really want to disparage the allurements of talking to a
scourge and ignoramus of the type that Signor X represents all

too vividly. He seemed sincere. Sitting opposite him in the crepuscular lobby of the Omnipotente, with my tape recorder—accompanist to history—hissing its absurdist sibilants, I couldn't help thinking, Ah, if only he could desist from his sins, we could have such a damned good time together!

Q. I'm wondering if you can explain your behavior, Signor X.

A. I don't—

Q. Not so fast, Signor X. Signor X, I have to admit I am a little surprised by your precipitousness. Do you really believe it's possible to explain away—and so hastily, at that—the infinite excruciations you have inflicted?

A. Excruciations? What excruciations?

Q. Signor X, forgive me if I retain a capacity for moral outrage. Perhaps I seem infantile. Or simply noxious. I hate to be noxious, especially since you've been so punctual, since you've bought me an *aperitivo* and so forth, but I have in mind, for instance, the time you—

A. I know what you are going to say, and it's completely untrue. *Basta!* I don't have to endure these questions, these vilifications, these reproaches, which are reported so often and ad infinitum in your newspaper.

A. *Con permesso,* Signor X, are you or are you not a Fascist hyena?

A. Of course not! Don't be silly! What a calumny! Do I look like a hyena?

Q. I think you do, Signor X. It frightens you to hear that—yes, it frightens you.

A. Nothing frightens me. For me, it's not at all a question of fear.

Q. Very well. We don't have to bicker.

A. The main question can be adduced from one point. I am a father. Italians like that. Italians like fathers—Carlo Ponti, the Holy Father, and so on. Maybe the father isn't always such a good father, maybe he is a despot and so forth, but he's in the right. In short, a father.

Q. Yes, yes, but tell me this: If I drove slivers of bamboo under your fingernails and forced you to choose between having a coffee with Jesus Christ and having a coffee with Hitler, which would you choose?

A. It's obvious, neither one. But why do you have these fantasies of persecuting me? The thought is father to the deed, when all's said and done. Yet am I such a bad man?

Q. Shall we say I'm wondering, Signor X, if you are a happy man. Are you a happy man, Signor X?

A. Happy? *Dio mio,* little girl, let's be realistic. For one moment let's get something straight. Happiness is the father of unhappiness.

Q. How many times you keep returning to this word "father," Signor X. One would almost say you have had that word on the brain during this interview!

A. So are we finished so soon? Now do me one favor. Say it.

Q. Say what?

A. You know what I mean. Say it.

Q. As you like. "You're the top, you're the Colosseum."

A. You remembered. Thank you.

Q. Thank *you,* Signor X. Thank you very much, Daddy.

A Man Called José

There was a swift, almost liquid beauty to the Neva River yesterday, as you looked at it from the seedy little bench on the Prospekt Parkway in Leningrad, but Ivan and Igor and two to three thousand other Russians were not there to see it now.

They were in Cuba, wearing uniforms and marching and being photographed from U-2s by nice kids from neighborhoods in the Bronx or Queens or the Silk Stocking District. Kids with mothers and fathers whose eyes had been red and swollen with tears of pride when their sons graduated from USAF Intelligence Aerial Reconnaissance School on the upper West Side.

And now, 10,000 miles away from anywhere, the Neva rolled on in gaudy indifference.

Igor and Yuri and the rest of them had been talked about by an American President on all the TV sets and written up in stories by American journalists in the papers. The presses still rolled with indifferent swiftness now, and images flickered still on the grayish 22-inch screens in the bars on Bruckner Boulevard and the political clubs on Mulberry Street and on the imported Sony color Trinitrons along Lexington Avenue, but Ivan and his comrades did not know it. All they knew was marching and gaudy uniforms and overhead the U-2s passing once in a while in arcs of swollen pride.

A crumpled Silva Thins cigarette pack and a couple of barbecue-flavored-chorizo wrappers blew along the Boulevard Astoria in Havana yesterday with a proud gaudiness that had a kind of beauty, but Murphy and Santini and Franklin and the others were not there to see it now.

They were in the bars that line the Whitestone Bridge and the Harlem River and the Belt Parkway exit of the Van Wyck Expressway. They had come in swift, remorseless cars, and some of them had even come proudly on foot from the homes not so far away.

The homes bought with V.A. loans.

At one of the bars, the floor was littered with sawdust and there were shabby scrunched-up Frito bags and a sad array of half-empty glasses on the worn brownish wood of the bar. Reflected in the mirror was a gaudy litter of half-full liquor bottles.

They were all there. All the men who had gone to school and gotten jobs and now were damned ready to have a couple of Millers or Buds. And now there was a reporter at a corner of the bar.

"How about this Soviet brigade thing?" he said.

"What the hell," said Murphy, and his voice sounded hollow and indifferent and scared for a man whose people had been immigrants a long time ago.

"Who is this guy?" said Santini.

The guy's name is Leonid Brezhnev and his name is Fidel Castro and by any name he is a gutless thug. But nobody wanted to name names in this neighborhood.

And who could blame these men with the vacant eyes for never having heard of Leonid Brezhnev and Fidel Castro? For never having read *Uncle Vanya* and *Proletarian Revolution and the Renegade Kautsky* and *Highlights of the Bolshoi?*

They were thinking about whether to shoot some white people or some black people and wondering if any of it would really make a difference.

The reporter said some of this, and now a heavy man stood up and started to roll up the sleeves of the gaudy white shirt that was tucked despairingly into his gray pants at the waist.

If you believed the stories that were going around, an American President on TV had said long weeks ago that he received assurances from the Soviets that the brigade in Cuba was no combat brigade. That it was just for show. Just "a manifestation of Moscow's dominance of Cuba."

For all these men knew, that might be the truth.

But that didn't mean they weren't going to be able to defend themselves against it. Or against any other manifestation.

These people could teach something about manifestations to Brezhnev and Castro and their palookas in Moscow and Havana. Had Brezhnev ever seen a Holy Name parade on 125th Street? Had Castro ever seen a bar mitzvah at the Mineola Democratic Club, with Bessie Smith shouting her heart out and the gaudy platters of spiedini and the ward captains flourishing their tally sheets? Had Ivan and Rudi and Mischa ever seen a heavy man rolling up the sleeves of his white shirt?

On the tacky little glass-and-metal Zenith above the bar, somebody on a *Kojak* rerun said, "I've had it!"

Nobody really knew what would happen now, and that was the truest measure of a democracy.

Meanwhile, outside in the indifferent darkness, here were swollen politicians crouched squabbling over a piece of white paper with remorseless black printing on it, called SALT II.

It was time for everybody to go home.

Murphy and Krupnick and Franklin would show the reporter some moves and then go out in despair and slap their Dodge Darts and Toyota Coronas into gear.

Igor and Boris would march and be photographed and never read *The Portable Thomas Jefferson* or *The Postman Always Rings Twice.*

And a man called José would be forgotten.

It was over now.

Except for those of us who had a column to get out. And perhaps that was the greatest injustice of all.

Petticoat Power

"I find it very helpful to attend business meetings under an alias."
—Estelle Crinoline, Vice-President in Charge of
Assistants at a major conglomerate

Nowadays, the fair sex functions in a managerial capacity in U.S. businesses at every level, from the lowly assistant vice-president to the topflight vice-presidential assistant. The "gal Friday" has long since become a full-fledged deckhand, and the "steno" has made it into the ranks of flunkies to the powers that be. It is even estimated that women constitute a percentage of all egress-level managers. If you are one of them, the Sword of Damocles is beginning to swing your way, and you will soon see the time when women are promoted over better-qualified minorities and minors.

As a result, the ambitious female of the species need no longer turn furtively to the so-called execu-cosmetology schools, which dispense little more than a bow tie and a fountain pen. The following guide, based on information, should amply fill the needs of women and would-be women in business.

WHAT IS BUSINESS?

The field of business is so manifold that no single article can hope to do more than this one. In the main, however, all businesses are basically alike in their approach, and women would do well to remember the generally uniform surface of the masculine brain even as it offers openings for women.

WHAT MAKES AN EXECUTIVE?

A good executive must first be equipped with the tools of the trade. Top male execs know well the necessity for carrying in their possession at all times some form of credentials (the service revolver, tire iron, or Sword of Damocles). Women must not shrink faintheartedly from doing likewise. Moreover, credentials exist to be used. Show the credentials at once when approaching a colleague. This display lends an air of importance to the encounter; the colleague more readily believes that the meeting is a serious matter, not just casual chitchat.

The executive is also versed in the "hidden language" of the biz-ocracy—the fundamentals that touch every swivel chair in every corridor of power. The General Business Code, prescribed for all commercial transactions in the U.S., is transmitted by breast-pocket-handkerchief semaphore (and may in future be modernized to adopt feminine visual apparatus—e.g., the hairnet). The seven basic signals are:

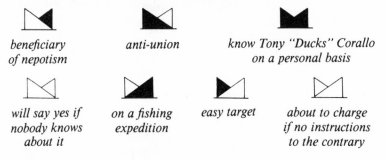

beneficiary of nepotism	*anti-union*	*know Tony "Ducks" Corallo on a personal basis*

will say yes if nobody knows about it	*on a fishing expedition*	*easy target*	*about to charge if no instructions to the contrary*

With the influx of Milady into the executive "sweet," new terms are gradually being added:

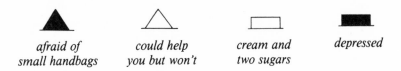

afraid of small handbags	*could help you but won't*	*cream and two sugars*	*depressed*

THE MENTOR

Having mastered these skills, the she-male in business will be served just as well—indeed, better—by attaching herself to a mentor. Every single business, no matter how similar to another, is completely different, and only through a mentor can you learn how mentorship itself works in your chosen field.

A mentor is a man who has reached a ranking position of awesome responsibility at the office; is richly dedicated to home, wife, and children; is actively involved in demanding community and leisure duties; and thus is ideally suited to spend long hours guiding a female co-worker through the intricacies of business.

The mentor is not to be confused with other paternal figures in the company, such as the doctor, proctor, loner, factor, drummer, exterminator, or mortgage shark.

The principal technique involved in finding a mentor is the stakeout. Mentors tend to gravitate toward specific loci of power, such as the shredder room. Keep a diary of their movements. (Entries should be made concurrently or afterward, never before.) Not untypical is the woman who staked out a deserted band shell, tailed the first man who appeared, and eventually followed him to his corporate headquarters, where he taught her how to build a car with her bare hands.

There are four types of mentors. As shown in the following transcriptions of videotaped experiences by distaff mentorees A, B, C, and D, each type of mentor has his characteristic way of showing you the rope:

TYPE 1—INFERENTIAL

A: Good morning, Bob.

MENTOR: What in the *hell* are you wearing?

A: Just a ... a simple jumpsuit with laminated pongee undercuffs, layered with a . . . a Bavarian vest and a Ralph Lauren cow blanket.

(*Mentor laughs contemptuously.*)

A (*confidence seeping into her voice*): I'm grateful for the advice, Bob.

TYPE 2—INSINUATIONAL

B: Have a nice weekend, Jack?

(*Mentor stares in a repelled manner at her coiffure.*)

B: Is something wrong with my hair?

MENTOR: If you choose to think so.

B: I'll get on it right away. And . . . Jack? (*In a newly assertive tone*) Well . . . thanks.

TYPE 3—MANIFESTATIONAL

C: I have those dioxin reports, Dick.

(*Mentor leans across desk, rips the tacky costume jewelry from her throat and wrists, and tosses it disgustedly into wastebasket.*)

C (*effectively*): Deemed it inappropriate, huh? Say no more.

TYPE 4—VERBAL

D: Morning, Ted.

MENTOR: You make a better door than a window.

D: Sorry. Did you see the *Times?*

MENTOR: Is the Pope Catholic?

D: Well . . . since it says the bond market has rallied—

MENTOR: Get off my ear.

D: —if we take into account the spillover effect from Wednesday's—

MENTOR: Can the tripe.

D: —and the new Treasury bonds' gain of—

MENTOR: Save your wind—you might want to go sailing sometime.

D: —then the prime rate—

MENTOR: That *rates* a hee-haw!

D: —but the Federal Reserve—

MENTOR: Hang crape on your nose—your brains are dead.

D: —may indicate that the tax-exempt sector is—

MENTOR: What are you—foggy in the upper story?

D: —I mean, now that the pace of new issues—

MENTOR: Go hire a hall.

D: Are you—you know—annoyed about something?

MENTOR: Pull in your head—here comes a termite.

D (*breaking out in "executive pattern" rash statistically linked to lateral thinking*): Gee, I guess I do need a manicure. 'Preciate the grooming tip!

With the confidence you will gain through this type of inter-action with a mentor, you will soon be able to take risks with-out fear of mistakes. Let's suppose you wish to offer a sugges-tion about some minor aspect of business practice:

Sample dialogue:

YOU: I was thinking, why don't we—

MENTOR: No.

YOU: But—

MENTOR: No. Go on, you were doing marvellously.

YOU: Oh, O.K. Wouldn't it make sense if we have a weekly—

MENTOR: No, absolutely not. Good girl, keep it up.

YOU: I mean, once a week, if each department—

MENTOR: *Jee-zus!* I told you, it's completely out of the question. Here, let's trade places and I'll show you how to do this.

YOU: I think I already know how to do it.

MENTOR: Of course you do. And you were doing beautifully, which is why you need someone to show you an alternative way of doing it.

YOU: Did I make a mistake?

MENTOR: Don't think about your mistakes. Don't ever think about your mistakes. Don't dwell on your mistakes. You'll make plenty of mistakes, but by no means dwell on them.

YOU: Right. Then let me put it this way. I want to restructure this company from the ground up. Just take a moment of your time, if you will, and imagine. In the mail room, raw lean-bodied youngsters, a future chairman of the board perhaps among them, learn the business from the bottom by democratically sodomizing each other in an atmosphere of interracial harmony and union solidarity. Thus prepared for the elevator ascent, to the strains of sense-quickening Muzak they steer from floor to floor their rattling mail carts of communiqués and memos proposing urgent trysts, many with nymphs from a typing pool awakened en masse by affairs with a vice-president whose blazing rise from the Harvard Business School to a position of line command has been short-circuited by a reputation for insatiable erotic appetites. The day begins for the accounting department, too, as hot numbers are speculated upon with mathematical frankness. Everywhere shirtsleeves are rolled up to expose wrists and forearms of unbearably breathtaking virility; panty hose are stripped off so that bare toes may frolic in the nap of the industrial carpeting. Smart pigskin briefcases and brown paper bags alike pop open to reveal black nylon corselets and posing straps, and aesthetically pleasing new birth-control devices, each a product of the newly stirring giant of American technology. By midmorning, as the refreshment wagon tinkles its merry news, quenching fruit juices are sought, caffeine and sugar renounced as redundant stimulants to surging metabolisms. Hands clutch atop reports and blueprints, limbs mingle upon varnished teak conference tables. By noon, sustenance is welcome; home-cooked box-lunch fare is contributed potluck style to the menu of the penthouse executive dining room, where one and all are served by Irish waiters and waitresses, whose rosy-cheeked charms are dispensed as a last course along with the claret. Restored, the staff returns to a worthwhile afternoon of disassembling the structures of power, once again tearing off collar stays and execu-length socks, T-shirts and work boots, with equal-opportunity abandon. The switchboard is as abuzz with interoffice calls for transvestites as a Weimar nightclub, while the computers, engineered for sexy problem-solving by a vanguard élite, are programmed to insert pornographic passages into the briefs of the lawyers, who, thus cast adrift on the uncertain seas of obscenity rulings, fall into confusion and disarray, incapacitated in their campaign to stifle creative urges with their lackey caution. Nepotistic marriages, too, are crumbling under the stress; bourgeois property-owning middle managers and hypocrite artists are selling their exurban retreats and gentrified lofts, reserving motel rooms convenient to the office. As desk lamps are turned this way and that to warm bare flesh, heat melts the grease that has eased the way of sycophants and bootlickers, who, losing their purchase on the success ladder, plunge into the communal endeavor on an equal footing. By late afternoon, all are gathered at the interdepartmental meeting, where brainstorming fully liberates the libido in service of the intellect, culminating in a heady explosion of honest labor. Well exhausted, the satisfied work force contemplates the wreckage of a numbing and exploitative system. Rivalries have been diverted into life-giving channels, oppressive authority has been leveled by the sway of desire, and the stultifying lock-march of corporate sameness has been diversified into a thousand different positions.

MENTOR: You're fired.

What Makes Them Tick

.... there are three aspects of the Presidential
campaign: one, what a candidate thinks about the
issues . . . ; two, what [he] has to say about what
he would do for the country . . . ; three, what
makes him tick.
—Senator Howard Baker, February 20, 1980

REPRESENTATIVE JOHN ANDERSON

In theory, propulsion is effected by droplets of condensed vapor, which adhere to a wooden-pole support until their potential energy is released, causing the blade to cut the hairs close to the follicles. The works are oiled daily with an ounce of butter cut into pea-size dots.

GOVERNOR EDMUND G. BROWN, JR.

Tiny micro-organisms affixed to the host go busily about their job of decomposition. The nitrogen thus liberated is used to flavor soybeans and other legumes, which are in turn recycled to the host as an energy source. When this system temporarily closes down, the host can be plugged into a direct-current circuit until the next phase.

GEORGE BUSH

Momentum, either linear or rotary, is imparted to a claw hammer by the circulation of quantities of displaced libido. The containment vessel sleeps six to eight.

PRESIDENT JIMMY CARTER

The central cavity is filled with natural uranium, which is constantly scanned by a Zeiss optical system. Random fluctuations of electrons are controlled by meditation, and the dark clouds of ash vented from the abyss are borne away by high winds. The apparatus as a whole can be swung in various directions, as it swivels about its main pivot.

SENATOR EDWARD M. KENNEDY

Small sprocket wheels pull the film off the feed reel and feed it to the takeup reel. In time, it reaches the sound head. The device is capable of transmitting coded information, in twelve-track Dolby, to surface facilities as far away as forty feet.

RONALD REAGAN

The clockwork drive, of the type developed in the first half of the nineteenth century, has been granulated and introduced through a hopper into the chamber, which has been well swabbed to remove powder fouling. For safety, the muzzle has been equipped with a warning signal. Engineers have not actually been able to get this model to tick yet, but with proper maintenance it may be struck manually to sound the quarter hour.

More Mathematical Diversions

1. ANTE UP

Coins have fascinated mathematicians for almost four thousand years. These baffling theoretical symbols, with their entertaining numerical properties, afford us many impromptu parlor tricks. This one was called to my attention by Y. Andropov, of Princeton, Nev. It employs ordinary silver pocket change, and never fails to elicit cries of disbelief when performed in company.

In the presence of two or more ordinary guests, lay out ten coins in a horizontal row on a flat-topped table. Ask a guest to tally the number values of the coins and record the combined value on a sturdy piece of paper. For the next 365 days, distract the guests with Frightening Matchstick Conundrums (Volume I). Then take the number on the paper and multiply it by the annual rate of inflation (available from any magicians' supply shop). Subtract the sum from the original number. Confoundingly, the probability that the result coincides with or is greater than the original number is 1/1,000,000, or .0001 percent.

The trick is ridiculously easy to understand once it is understood, and lays bare the very essence of the scientific method. It uses what Leibnitz called a "brain teaser." Astoundingly, the probability curve remains exactly the same if you cheat by trying to sell the piece of paper as a municipal bond. However, there is quite a pretty way to improve the odds in your favor by beginning with zero coins or the new nondenominational coins.

2. SEVEN BUGS

One of the classic mathematical fallacies was immortalized by William Wordsworth in his "On the Extinction of the Venetian Republic, 1802":

> Seven bugs each sought a mate
> From inside their own huddle;
> Yet none would woo another's date,
> So how were they to cuddle?
>
> "There's not much sense in grievin',"
> Said One, and gave a nod;
> "Let odd consort with even,
> And even pair with odd."
>
> So Six and Three went out to tea,
> And Five took Four to wife;
> One and Two kept company,
> And Seven took its life.

Addendum:

An ingenious resolution of this problem has been proposed by Dr. Werner Frye, of the Institute for Advanced Idling, who writes: "If each bug paired with a transfinite number, senseless tragedy might be averted."

3. THE MAZE OF VENUS

There is nothing mysterious about speech; it is merely a way of expressing thoughts without having to write them down. Yet the incredible verbal sequence known to logicians as the Maze of Venus quickly dispels the illusion that spoken language is a plausible means of communication. Here is the classical formulation of this sequence:

A: I don't think you want to see me more often.
B: That's not true.
A: Then you do want to see me more often.
B: I didn't say that. I just don't *not* want to see you more often.

Also known as the Paradox of Don Giovanni, this problem has long intrigued philosophers of science. The difficulties become clear if we let T represent the outer limits of A's tolerance, and $t^{\pm x}$ the measurable tenuousness of the relationship. Chess genius Pauline Morph's fatal attempt to extrapolate a boardplay solution (see "Mate in Five," *Science for Women,* May 1912) proved only that the Maze of Venus defies logical analysis.

4. JERKAGONS

Jerkagons are paper polygons, made by folding rectangular NASA payroll checks. They have the delightful property of changing shape when their edges are jerked in a particular way. Jerkagons were discovered by Dr. Yves St. Laurent, the French astrophysicist. St. Laurent's jerkagon can be manipulated so that it reveals three different faces. (See "The Three Faces of Yves," *Journal of Stereoisomers and Paper Games,* Summer, 1966.) He has set forth the principles of jerkagation in a mathematical proof of exquisite elegance, printed on off-white crêpe de Chine.

You can make a jerkagon quite easily. Fold check as shown in *Fig. 1.*

Figure 1

Now grasp your jerkagon by any two edges and give it a sharp
jerk, of the kind absurdly simple to describe as sort of an im-
ploded tremor. As if by magic, your jerkagon will assume one
of three possible shapes. (See *Figs. 2–4.*)

Figure 2   Figure 3

Figure 4

Addendum:

After my article about jerkagons appeared in the August
1975 *Scientific Whimsician,* I received the following corre-

spondence from Prof. Lance Mars, of Canaveral, Calif.:

"From way over here at another coordinate on this tiny hunk of stuff we call the Earth, I am prompted to report a curious incident which suggests that the properties of the jerkagon may be stunning and awesome beyond our wildest dreams. Early in October, I was driving south with my family, on my way to meet with a bunch of stuffy and unimaginative colleagues. While passing through an especially banal landscape in Georgia, I decided to use my very large brain to amuse my very small son. Pulling up beside what looked like a peanut thicket, I took from my wallet a canceled check for $125, folded it into a jerkagon, and told the boy how to manipulate it. He gave it a couple of dutiful tweaks and then flung it out of the window, into what looked like a peanut thicket, and demanded a doll.

"Within a matter of weeks, the national press had started to report the existence of someone named 'Jimmy Carter,' calling him 'an enigma' who had 'come out of nowhere.' Since physicists are in agreement that it is impossible for matter to 'come out of nowhere,' unless 'nowhere' is merely a word we use to mean a somewhere which we disapprove of, I do not hesitate to draw the controversial conclusion that 'Jimmy Carter' did indeed come out of somewhere, and that the somewhere which he came out of was my jerkagon.

"I now choose to speculate freely. Does the jerkagon's timespace, awesome and far-out as we may now surmise it to be, teem with intelligent life? Does it teem with billions and billions of teeth? How many more 'Jimmy Carters' await nothing more than the twiddle of a child's fingers to be projected into our national political life? Is 'Jimmy Carter' an extraterrestrial, and if he is an extraterrestrial is he Constitutionally disqualified from holding elective office on this planet? If these boggling possibilities don't put things in perspective, what will?"

5. ORTHO

This diverting game, known to many a schoolgirl in its traditional pencil-and-paper form, is now available in a manufactured version, designed and marketed by the Dutch inventor
Piet Heineken. Ortho makes use of a perforated plastic case
containing twenty-one disc-shaped counters. Play begins on
Day 1, when the player takes the first counter. Thereafter, any
combination of moves is either "safe" or "unsafe" (as binary
analysis will easily show). For example, in the common "1, 2,
3, 5" game, the player forgets to employ a counter on Day 4,
thus changing a "safe" position to an "unsafe" one. Any "safe"
position can be made "unsafe" by a wrong move. Since the
game depends entirely upon the player's memory, "rational"
strategies are impossible and there is no way to force a win.

The game's centuries-old popularity is attested to in many
historical references. The Phoenicians called it the Maze of
Venus, and it was familiar to the Anglo-Saxons as a pastime
called Preggers.

James at
an Awkward Age

The NBC-TV sitcom *James at 16,* canceled in 1978, will inevitably resume in a new format. Episode One, "Pop Quiz":

SEGMENT 1: *Interior, the Berkeley Institute, a boys' school in Newport, Rhode Island. The Reverend William Leverett has just finished lecturing on "Cicero as Such." Boys stream from the classroom into the hall. James and his only friend, Sargy, meet in front of James's locker.*

SARGY: James, my man! (*They shake hands.*) Isn't Leverett something else?

JAMES: As to what, don't you know? else he *is*—! Leverett is of a weirdness.

SARGY: Say, my man, what's going down?

JAMES: Anything, you mean, different from what is usually up? But one's just where one *is*—isn't one? I don't mean so much in the being by one's locker—for it does, doesn't it? lock and unlock and yet all unalterably, stainlessly, steelily glitter—as in one's head and what vibes one picks up and the sort of deal one perceives as big.

SARGY: Oh, I wouldn't sweat it.

JAMES: If one might suppose that in the not sweating it one should become—what do you fellows call it?—*cool*—!

SARGY: You pull it off.

JAMES: Would I "pull off" anything, then?

SARGY: I didn't say *anything.*

JAMES: It's what, isn't it? *he* can say.

SARGY: Leverett?

JAMES: Oh, Leverett! All the same, I wonder about *his* idea of him—Leverett's.

SARGY: Him?

JAMES: Precisely! One's own father.

SARGY: They say your pop's, like, a friend of Emerson's.

JAMES: Ah, *they!* But if one's to belong, in the event, to a group of other kids, without giving the appearance—so apparent beyond the covering it, in any way, up—of muscling at all in—! And if, under pressure of an ideal altogether American, one feels it tasteless and even humiliating that the head of one's little family is not "in business"—!

SARGY: Too much! But hasn't your dad hung out with Greeley and Dana?

JAMES: Oh, "hung"—very much so. But we don't know, do you know? what he *does.*

SARGY: I heard your old man got it on in the—you know, the spiritual reformation of the forties and fifties.

JAMES: Yes, and yet, you see, Sargy, exactly what the heck, all the while, do you think, like, *is* he?

SEGMENT 2: *Interior, the Sweet Shoppe. James is alone at a table.* ENTER *his cousin Minny.*

MINNY: May I sit down at all?

JAMES: Oh, immensely!

(*Waitress comes over.*)

MINNY: Only, I guess, a Coke.

JAMES: Well, perhaps just a thing so inconsiderable as—the hamburger? Of a rarity?

MINNY: Anyway, see, could you help me maybe study on Saturday, you know, night?

JAMES: Would it be a, then, kept date? I mean, the charm of the thing half residing in the thing itself's having been determined in advance and, in consequence, all intentionally and easily and without precipitant hassle or bummer, taking finally, in fact, place?

MINNY: That's exactly what it would be kind of like.

(Waitress brings their orders. James takes a bite of his burger.)

JAMES: This is, on the whole roll, particularly not rare. And *you*—you so too stupendously are! I say—do you think I *had* better keep it?

MINNY: Our date?

JAMES: The little hamburger.

MINNY: If you're, I mean, *on* something—

JAMES: Oh, it's not, I swear—no way!—*drugs.* Unless *it's* one.

MINNY: The hamburger?

JAMES: No, the wondering, do you read me? in respect to *(despondently)* oh, wow! *him!*

SEGMENT 3: *Interior, James's house. James looks into the sitting room, where his brothers, Willy, Wilky, and Bob, and his sister, Alice, are gathered before dinner, chaffing each other. James goes down the hall and meets his mother.*

JAMES: Only *do* say, Mom, how I'm not to fail in the finding of him—

MOTHER: In his study. Hurry up, my dear—some of his Swedenborgians will be here soon.

(James goes to Father's study.)

FATHER: Come in, son. I was just corresponding with Carlyle and Mill.

JAMES: Ah, but it's all so quite buggingly on *that* point, if I might for a moment be allowed to be prefatory no less than interrogatory, and interrogatory no less than up, as it were, front, with regard to your little interlocutor's—that is to say, myself's—becoming, in the not grossing the other boys altogether out at least as much as in the not blowing it in getting what they nowadays call "along" with girls, in any way proficient—and oh! if Minny might feel me up, do you see? to *her* level—that now, while I'm too almost hot to have your answer—and am I not, though, in my own pyrotechnics, fairly cooking!—would I put to you my minuscule question:

MOTHER (*appearing in doorway*): The Swedenborgians are here.

JAMES: *There* pokes at me the stick, as well as beckons to me the carrot, of acceleration. Oh, Dad!—if I may "keep the ball in play"—you work, you *do* work, I guess—do you?—that's my question. Do tell me. I dare say *you* know what it is you, um, "do"? Or only give me the small dry potato-chip-crumb of a hint. For if it's even a matter of your not declining to say what you aren't, then doesn't it follow, don't you see? that you needn't say what you *are?*

FATHER: Why, son! Say I'm a philosopher, say I'm a seeker for truth, say I'm a lover of my kind, say I'm an author of books if you like. Or best of all, just say I'm a student.

SEGMENT 4: *The Sweet Shoppe. James is sitting at a table with Sargy and Minny.*

JAMES: *We're* all of us students, aren't we? And if each of us is to be all convivially "in," then *he* must naturally be!

SARGY: Ah, my man—all *right!*

JAMES: Yet one *has* seen great big grown-up dudes, well encumbered, one might surely have thought, with the inertest of ponderousnesses, put, by one's little crowd, down as positively not, on the social scales as rigged by *them,* sufficiently heavy.

MINNY: *I* haven't. I mean, we all, like, what's the difference? you know, speak the same language.

JAMES: But there *he* is!

(*James's father enters Sweet Shoppe and sits down at their table, where Minny helps him with his homework. James, in a sudden huff, goes to the jukebox and plays "Come On, Baby, Don't Hang Fire."*)

NEXT WEEK: A harrowing mix-up occurs at a drive-in movie until it is discovered that James and his father are both named Henry.

Teaching Poetry
Writing to Singles

I had the idea to teach more kinds of people to write poetry as a result of two previous books of mine: *I Taught Republicans to Write Poetry* and *How to Teach the Writing of Poetry to Fashion Coordinators.* I thought of singles because of an interesting hour I had spent reading my own poems at a singles bar called Ozymandias II, and because of many other hours, much less happy ones, I had spent before my marriage as a visitor to another singles bar, Nick's Roost, where there were no activities of that kind going on.

I asked the owners of Ozymandias II, my friends Ozzie and Mandy Dias, to arrange for the class. I had four students, and we met once, on a Friday at midnight, at the big table in front. Like the others in the crowded room, most of the four were in their twenties, thirties, forties, and fifties. Some of them wore glasses. One worked for an escort agency, one was a hayride organizer, another a fashion coordinator, another a Republican. The singles bar gave these people a feeling of meetability, but none had ever written poetry there, and none, I think, would have done so without me.

I started the class by saying what I was going to do was get them to write words in lines of uneven length on a piece of paper (I didn't want to scare them with the formal term "poem") and then I would write a book about how much I had helped them. The students were not in the habit of sitting and hearing something like this explained. Some were so distracted that they could only talk in incomplete sentences, such as "What the—?!" Others stared nervously at the TV screen above the bar, where the final minutes of some kind of sports event seemed to be going on. I said that writing words in lines of uneven length on a piece of paper was not the hard thing that many people think. I said how could it be hard if I was going to teach it to them? I was sure I could give them the mastery of literary form and metaphor so lacking in singles-bar life. I said I knew they had all been single since childhood and I could see how this might make them feel "unmarried" and "on their own," but I said John Milton and Vachel Lindsay and James Dickey had all been single at one time or another and that writing words in lines of uneven length on a piece of paper had helped them to stop running.

I said the first thing we would do would be a collaboration. I knew the students had all gone on a singles bicycling tour of the Wye River in England five years before, so I said I want everyone to remember that trip and think of a sentence about it. Something you saw. Or an outfit you wore. Or a feeling you had about time passing and your not being married yet and having to go on bicycle tours to meet somebody. I'll write down everyone's sentence and put them together, I said, and we'll have words in lines of uneven length on a piece of paper.

At first the students were puzzled. "We went there, that's all." "I remember we did different stuff." "And bicycling." Then William said, "O.K. A double vodka, please. Five years have passed; five summers, with the length of five long winters!" This was a good start, I said, especially the dramatic "frame" made by "O.K. A double vodka, please," as if the lines were being said casually to someone by someone sitting in a bar or tavern.

Then Ezra spoke up: "And again I hear these waters, rolling from their mountain springs with a soft inland βροδοδάκτυλος." This was better than I had expected, but the poem was getting a false-sounding jig-jigging rhythm, and I said for the students not to worry about academic gimmicks such as meter. I also said try to get in more of your own personal feelings and hangups. I said for instance I remember when I was in high school I worried a lot about my bike getting rusty.

It was Emily's turn: "Once again do I behold these steep and lofty cliffs, that on a wild secluded scene impress thoughts: the soul selects her own scene, but you meet more eligible guys by going out and partying rather than staying at home." I said the repetition of "scene" was nice, it gave a nice feeling of repetition.

At this point William got very agitated and said we were ruining "his" idea. I said all right, you do the next part, but I pressed him to put in more details from his own experience as a single—the very details that he seemed most reluctant to put in, maybe because he thought they were "stupid." He continued: "The day is come when I again socialize, taking a nice girl to dinner and a show, and view the floor show and the salad bar, which at this season, with its unripe fruits, is clad in one green hue, and lose myself 'mid men and women, who have different attitudes toward sex."

Quite soon the students felt they had enough words in lines of uneven length on a piece of paper. I read the results back to them and said what they had written was a poem. I asked them to think of a title. They decided the poem was really about working out the problems of writing a poem, so they called it "Working Out at the Wye."

I then said to do individual poems. Writing a poem all by yourself is something that nobody can do with you, and this is a special problem for people who are already panicked about being alone, such as so-called singles. I say "so-called" because the words "single," "bachelorette," etc., may be thought to apply to people's *imaginations,* and they do not. The power to see the world as a configuration of couples linked inextricably in Holy Matrimony is the possession of everyone.

I told the students that one of the main problems poets have is what to write about. I said this was a really hard problem if you were lonely and in a studio apartment and had to go out to a bar to seek some grotesque mockery of human contact. But I said that in a poem you can be somebody else, you can even be *two* people. I said for everyone to start their own poem with "Let us..." The "us" in the poem could do anything: get married, have a huge church wedding with a flower girl and a page boy, sit down and talk over family finances—anything.

The most popular "Let us..." poem was Tom's:

Let us go then, you and me,
When the weekend is spread out for us to see
Like a roommate bombed out of his gourd on the pool table....
Oh, do not ask, "You said you were *who?*"
Let us go to the free luau.

In the room the women come and go
Talking of someone who might be tall and share their enthusiasm
   for theater.

I praised Tom's poem, saying it might seem silly to a lot of people but to me it gave a nice sociable feeling, the sounds of nice people talking to each other. I said there were many more things having to do with the five senses that could be in a poem, like colors. I said for instance when I was a boy I had a dog named Rusty. I said close your eyes and take a swallow of beer and say what color it reminds you of. They answered. "Black." "Beer color." "Black." "Blackish." After this exercise,

Ezra wrote his "Little Black Book" poem:

Hang it all, Mark Cross,
there can be but the one little black book. . . .
Under black leather dress, lithe daughter of telephone directory . . .

I said noises could be in a poem. I threw a beer stein on the
floor and asked what word the noise sounded like. "Bunk."
"Drunk." "Black." "Bash." Right away Emily wrote something down and gave it to me:

I dreamt I was a Key Club,
Select Fraternity.
At night the eligible Men
All had a Bash at me.

I said that in a poem you can compare things in goofy ways.
Compare something small to something yellow, something big
to something you don't know the name for, something married
to something legally separated. William later told me that this
idea made him write his nice poem that starts:

Shall I compare thee to your place or mine?

I was surprised when it was 4 A.M., closing time at Ozymandias
II. The students were still quite excited and said could they stay
for a few minutes after hours because they wanted to collabo-
rate on one final poem, a poem for me. They made me go into
the john while they wrote, and when I came back they were
laughing. The poem was this:

Thank you, this has been as much fun as a free trip
To Aspen—only I can't ski and anyhow I'd probably break some-
    thing
In several places, crack! crack! crack!

Gosh, thanks, I simply feel as if you gave me a raunchy souvenir
    T-shirt from the
Annual Bachelor Rally—quite an icebreaker, but I already have one.

By the way, thank you for this night like a bag of yellow Doritos, the
  name reminds me of a dog I once heard of named Doris
But I'm on a diet of blue and of purple.

Thank you for an experience similar to drinking tee Martoonis,
Which I could compare to those other clear drinks that I can hardly
  be expected to remember the name of. Oh—water!

Listen, really, we all thank you for teaching us that looks aren't
  everything, even in a poem.

I said they had learned a whole lot and it was a really nice
poem, one that gave a strong feeling of niceness.

The Stylish
New York Couples

These four couples have different names and faces, but they have one thing in common—a strong tendency to appear in articles of this kind, because they are fashion individualists. One couple may prefer an eclectic style, another retro-amalgam, another mongrel revival, and another hybrid-*retrouvé,* yet each couple stands on his and her own as a single, unique personality. They show that to be one of a kind, you have to be one of a pair.

Artist Marie Bane (25) and collector Morton Braine (30) dress in simple, bold fabric wrappings—colorful bolts and mill ends layered directly onto the skin with rubber cement. "We call it Yardage Formalism," says Morton, whose current project is winding all the furniture in their Tribeca penthouse with colored thread inherited from his grandparents, Coco Chanel and David Belasco. Adds Marie, "When Julian Schnabel's show sold out, I thought mine would, too, but then it didn't."

Her clothes: Scalamandré, Museum of Tissues (Lyons), Taipei silkworm farms. Mad Frisson and Warren Beatty for shoes.
His clothes: Porthault, Einstein Moomjy. Galerie du Sabot (Brussels) for shoes.

Interests: Oneiromancy, vacuuming up bits of thread, intaglio hunting, reading.

Restaurants: Chive, La Petite Bière, Imperial Musk-Polyp, Charlie's Bum Steer, La Tricoteuse, Folie à Deux (Paris).

Neither William nor Mary Molding (both 88) has bought any clothing in over 50 years. They feel that they have "subsumed fashion under the category of pure tradition." Both dress exclusively in what Mary calls "lateral hand-me-downs: I wear Moldie's old clothes and he wears mine." Real-estate collector William likes to wheel and deal on their Park Avenue triplex telex in a Schiaparelli cocktail dress, and relaxes later in "nothing at all except a dab of vintage Shocking on pulse points." For Mary, founder of the Ghetto Repair League and president of the Don't Be Beastly to Congress Committee, living well still means "a dinner coat always"—the one handmade for her husband in 1909 by Eugene V. Debs.

Her clothes: His.

His clothes: Hers.

Interests: Reading, telephoning, telescopes.

Restaurants: "It is impossible to go out." Entertain close friends at amusing dinners famous for including musk-polyps in every course.

Annabella Carissima ("Pat") von Patina (49), a Milan-born architect, and Stanley Sohoux (18), former collector, have shaped each other's design sensibilities in the ongoing process of gradually removing everything they own from their fabulous 40,000-square-foot loft in the bone-meal district. "I'm a bit big on minimalism," says Pat, "but Stan is completely his own man and has *kept* one or two little *objets* instead of relying on me to throw them away." Stan sometimes wears all his clothes at once, carrying his personal possessions in the pockets, "so the spatial interpenetrations of the open-plan closets can be kept unobstructed." Pat sticks to one designer for clothes and keeps her efficient wardrobe stored flat behind the ceiling in the crawlspace.

Her clothes: Ralph Racquet for Women. Warren Beatty and Mad
    Frisson for shoes.
His clothes: Ralph Racquet for Women for Men.
Interests: Medicinal-brandy tastings, oneiromancy. Visiting friends
    (Stan). Reading, intaglio disposal (Pat).
Restaurants: La Tricoteuse, Huis Clos, Chive, Imperial Musk-Polyp,
    Folie à Deux (Paris).

The proprietors of Chive, one of the most popular new dining places in town, Clive (35) and Olive (25) Alive are self-proclaimed "style immortals." Explains Clive, "By translating ourselves into commodities, we become abstract concepts of exchange; for that which hovers in a shop waiting to be bought is an immutable idea. As long as we are still for sale, we cannot be used." Everything in their East Side apartment has its price sticker—even the much-mended antique purse seine covering the walls, to which are pinned costly holograph pages from Richard Strauss's *Ariadne auf Naxos* and inexpensive crayon tracings of autumn leaves from their country estate ("Macy's" in Oxfordshire). The rare Sabayon carpet invites a visitor to lift it and explore the bargains beneath. Both Clive and Olive created their own wardrobes by stitching together labels bought in bulk at wholesale: "We transcend the material."

Her clothes: Calvin Mazuma, Yves Ducat, Vittorio Dinero, Simo-
    leon, Made of Money. Mad Frisson and Warren Beatty for shoes;
    cobbles her own boots from Levi's labels.
His clothes: Mach Wash Tumble Dry, Property of the Harvard Ath-
    letic Association, I.L.G.W.U., It Is Illegal to Remove This Tag.

Galerie du Sabot (Brussels) for shoes, Savile Row for sweatbands.
Interests: Collecting, reading, taking inventory.
Restaurants: Betamax of Athens, Imperial Musk-Polyp, Folie à
Deux (Paris).

Masterpiece Tearjerker

Our host, the famous Americophile, is reclining on a horsehair chaise longue—a replica of the one in the foyer of the men's lavatory at Waterloo Station. Beside him on a table are a lamp made from a cast of Lord Kitchener's torso and an exact reproduction of a water tumbler. He puts aside his book, forms a tepee with his fingers to signal transatlantic cordiality, and meets our eye.

HOST: Good evening, Yanks. We come now to the eight-hundred-fifty-seventh episode in our series *U and Non-U*, in which we follow the very human ups and downs of everyone in Britain in the years before, during, and after the First War. It was a time of pacifists and plum duff, of shirkers and scullery maids, of aesthetes and armament manufacturers, of White's and Boodle's (*pause; then, gravely*) and bombs.

Last time, of course, we saw Lord Randolph Crust committing a really disastrous gaffe by accidentally setting fire to Devonshire House while showing off his electrical Boer War set, Lytton Strachey receiving a letter from H. A. L. Fisher, and Lady Mary Crust getting herself into a peck of trouble by commencing an affair with a really unsuitable twelve-year-old schoolboy, Cecil Formalin. We come in now on Lady Mary, who has just returned from an outing with Cecil—an outing that was, as we shall see, something of a bust.

The year, 1910. Episode Eight Hundred Fifty-seven: "The Gathering Tantrum."

SCENE 1: *The morning room. Lady Mary is alone, weeping.* ENTER *her best friend, Lady Laura Fantod.*

LAURA: My dear, what's the dynamite?

MARY: It's too frightful! We chanced on one of Cecil's school friends, who insulted me in public. He said I put him in mind of a vulgar, common American woman!

LAURA: Which one?

MARY: Which American woman?

LAURA: Which friend of Cecil's?

MARY: Evelyn Wore, or Wall, or something. *Such* an unpleasant little party. This younger set! The old moral order seems to be smashing up all round us these days.

(ENTER *Hooting, the butler.*)

HOOTING: Excuse me, my lady, but I have just received word that the young mistress Viola is, er, arrested.

MARY: You're telling me my own daughter is a mental defective?

HOOTING: Arrested by the police, my lady. These suffragette carryings-on. The young mistress chained herself to Mr. Asquith.

LAURA: My dear, *quel* case of pickles! Viola will be forcibly fed in prison—and not on your splendid Mrs. Winkle's *rissoles.*

MARY: That girl never had much in the way of appetite. (*Becomes hysterical.*)

VOICEOVER: Starting this Friday, Beryl Simon (who plays Viola Crust) can be seen in the BBC's four-episode dramatization of the *Dictionary of National Biography,* along with these other actors and actresses who have been temporarily or permanently displaced from the plot of *U and Non-U:* Simon Graham (Captain Neville Crust, now a remittance man in Mombasa), Graham Glansdale (old Lord Roger Crust, dead), Sarah Pinch (Rosalind, mad), Derek Lamb (Reg, the chauffeur, sacked), and Rosalind-Beryl Graham (Nanny, on holiday with her sister in Reading).

SCENE 2: *An enormous spread (cakes on tiered plates, etc.) on several long tables in Lord Randolph's office at Whitehall. Lord Randolph and General Simon fFen-Nightingale are having tea.*

FFEN-NIGHTINGALE: Jolly decent five-o'clock they lay on here at Whitehall. (*Chews.*) Toad-in-the-hole, my favorite.

RANDOLPH: Spotted Dick, too. Very tasty, very tasty.

(ENTER *a young woman with an ineffably sad and beautiful face and superb carriage. She wears a shabby but meticulously pressed coat and skirt from Worth, and carries a tray of rock buns.*)

RANDOLPH: Put those— (*Does double take.*) Who are you?

WOMAN: Edith Bullock, sir. (EXITS *proudly.*)

RANDOLPH: Why the devil do you suppose a woman of that type is serving tea?

FFEN-NIGHTINGALE: Bit too fond of the old horizontal refreshment, I daresay. Now, you wanted to have a spot of chinwag, my boy?

RANDOLPH: Yes, it's this German—you know, thingy. Wireless message? I seem to have, you know—decoded it. And it looks like we're in for what-do-you-call-it. War. The thing is, something really colossal came up—quarrel with Mary—and I misplaced the message. The P.M. will have me on toast! I was, you see, so preoccupied about Mary. Poor old thing, she's been rippingly unselfish and patient. I haven't been a—you know— proper husband to her ever since—well, ever since I went off my onion about *you.* (*Breaks down.*) Y-you won't repeat any of this, will you?

FFEN-NIGHTINGALE: My dear boy, give me credit for some natural delicacy. And now let's look for that message. Trust bleeding Jerry to telegram at a time like this!

SCENE 3: *The Green Farm, Timworth, near Bury St. Edmunds. Exterior.* ENTER *Lytton Strachey, with valise. Knocks on door. Housemaid opens door.*

STRACHEY: I am Mr. Strachey. Mr. McCarthy asked me to spend the weekend.

HOUSEMAID: Mr. McCarthy is in Paris, sir.

STRACHEY: Oh. (*Business with valise*) Well, thanks all the same. Good day. (*Goes away wistfully.*)

SCENE 4: *The servants' hall at Eaton Place. Late afternoon. Mrs. Winkle, the cook, is scowling over her* Mrs. Beeton. *Dora, the parlormaid, is whittling new boot trees for Viola. Doris, the scullery maid, is attempting to poison herself because she is hopelessly in love with Mr. Bangers, purveyor of sausages to the Crust kitchen.* ENTER *Hooting.*

HOOTING: Doris! Whatever have you got in that best crystal decanter?

DORIS: Harsenic, Mr. 'Ooting. Oh, please, let me do meself in. I can't stand it no more!

HOOTING: Unrequired love and that, is it? Well, hard cheddar, my girl. The master and mistress are counting on you to remain here in this life, as a member of the staff. You do as you're told now, and put the kettle on. (*Doris slopes off to kitchen.*) And get your finger out! It's nearly teatime. (*Grumbles to self.*) That girl's as cunning as a dead pig.

DORA: Not 'alf!

(ENTER *Joseph, the footman.*)

HOOTING: And where might you have been, my lad?

JOSEPH: Just off for a pint of the old purko down at The Swan and Dead Pig.

HOOTING: You seem to be getting a tick independent for a mere thirty-year-old man, Joseph. Mark my words—

(ENTER *Lady Mary.*)

MARY: I *am* sorry—I don't quite know how to break this to all of you. I've been so preoccupied lately that I forgot to mention it. King Edward VII and Mrs. Pankhurst and Cosima Wagner are all coming to dinner. Rather soonish. Tonight, in fact. (*Hooting falls to the floor and displays the painstakingly researched symptoms of an apoplectic fit.*) Now, Hooting, we mustn't let down dear old H.R.H., must we? And you always manage *so* well.

HOOTING: Forgive me, my lady. . . . I'm done for . . . off to join the celestial poultry. . . . Carry on without me. . . . Mustn't let down standards . . . key to the cellar . . . the nought-three Haut-Brion. . . . (*Staff gamely stifles sobs.*)

MRS. WINKLE: Never you fear, Mr. 'Ooting, we'll do right proud by you. A lovely Aberdeen cutlet, I think—'e always loved my Aberdeen cutlet, 'e did, when 'e was Prince of Wales.

HOOTING: That's right . . . standards . . . oh, no, *the best decanter* . . . (*Dies.*)

HOST: Several days later, the King, too, was dead—reportedly of a bronchial condition. And with him the old moral order bit the dust. (*Cut to photograph of Big Ben.*) I remember as a boy hearing people say, in the streets, "Oh, pack it in with your old moral order." (*Cut to photographs of Dr. H. H. Crippen; a red grouse; Arthur Wing Pinero.*)

Next week, Joseph does a bunk with Lord Randolph's second-best railway shares; Vita Sackville-West invites Harold Nicolson to a dance (*cut to photograph of potted palm*); and much, much more.

And you can be sure that we haven't heard the last of Edith Bullock. I remember as a boy seeing ever so many Edith Bullocks at evening parties in my parents' house, where I lived. In the fashion of the time, they all wore long dresses and perfume and did their hair. I would sit on the stair landing and gaze down on them and wonder what it all *meant*. (*Smiles.*) Now, of course, we know.

Coming Apart at the Semes

Serenade

Why are we here? There are eighteen of us in one room, with bath. The room is locked from the outside and is unfurnished, except for low cushioned benches along the walls, where we sleep, and twenty-five Venetian-glass bonbon services. We wear at all times the regulation blue negligee, and most of our personal belongings have been confiscated, particularly those items good for hollow displays of independence: our horn-rims, compacts, step-ins, carryalls.

We arrived here, one by one, the night before last. We have not seen him since, the man we were taken by, yet so great is the power of his indifference that we are able to make only the smallest, most circumscribed movements, such as twining a strand of hair around one finger.

I was taken at midnight, in the garden near my kitchen door. I had gone out to investigate a sudden fear that something unusual would never happen to me, and there he was, in the dark, a figure. He was wearing either all black or all white—I could not be sure, for the authority of his form against the tangled, familiar shrubbery caused him to read as featureless surface and I was not able to tell whether he absorbed or reflected light. He carried a thin glittering object in one hand.

"What do you want?" I said.

He made no reply.

"Why so withdrawn?" I said.

With a savagery that bordered on total inattention, he said nothing.

"Fine!" I screamed. "Don't bother to draw me a diagram! You don't give a hoot about me! Well, for your information, you don't know anything about me yet! What do you want— the dance of the seven espadrilles? What is it you want?" (One partner always cares a little more than the other.)

I must have fainted then. What followed: The chloroformed hankie? The wrist bonds? Freedom glimpsed one last time through the black tulle curtains of a limousine rolling away? I can't remember. When I came to my senses, I was in a limousine with black tulle curtains, rolling away. No point in mincing words here: I was definitely not driving. To shirk the truth in one's own journal is like going to a dinner party and letting cigarette ash drift down one's décolletage and coming home afterward and saying to oneself, "Thank goodness I didn't let cigarette ash drift down my décolletage, and thank goodness, too, I have the courage not to deceive myself about it."

SUNDAY

So far, very little interaction among the women—only shared confusion and a growing consciousness that whoever bought these negligees paid for a designer name while settling for inferior materials and workmanship.

MONDAY

Today, our first discussion:

"What does he want?"

"He has no use for us. He doesn't like us."

"But he's kept us for three days."

"Maybe he believes in long engagements."

"He just wants us to play hard to get."

"Maybe it's a test. We guess what he wants."

"Outreach?"

"What if every one of us writes him a note explaining how fascinating she is?"

"What would you say?"

"Well, I'm not a good example."

"No way to talk. Besides, you're with me, we're with them, as an ensemble we have a certain geometric charm."

"Maybe he's a prude."

"Or a eunuch."

"Doubtful. From what little I saw . . ."

"He doesn't exactly have hair-trigger responses."

"If he loses interest this easily, he's going to dump us and import some new talent to leave alone. Younger talent, whose perfect breasts rise with equal curves on every side and equally terminate in their apexes, whose—"

"The way he ignores us—I see it as kind of a higher form of interest."

"What evidence do we have of that?"

"We're here, aren't we?"

WEDNESDAY

He's not rushing us: that's clever of him.

Why am I keeping this journal? (a) Because I am different. (b) Because I hold the conviction that as the centuries march on, and civilization advances, and the relations between men and women become more interesting on account of our not knowing, now, what they will be, women like me will be recognized as extraordinary marginal curiosities. (Such, I believe, is already the case in Scandinavia.) And yet, now that I am having an experience whose unusualness is a match for my own, I wonder: With seventeen other women inhaling the same privileged air, is this unusual *enough?*

MONDAY

Today we played "Lifeboat."

"O.K., you have ten survivors. The nun, the pregnant woman, the majorette, the ninety-year-old lady, the little girl, the waitress, the nurse, the robber—how many is that? Oh, and the little girl's mother and Helen Frankenthaler. Who do you throw off?"

"The robber is a man?"

"Yes. Come on. Which one?"

"You can't throw off the pregnant woman, because that's taking two lives instead of one. You can't throw off the little girl, because she has her whole life—"

"Is it a male nurse?"

"No."

"Throw off the waitress."

"Elitism."

"Throw off Frankenthaler. What's art anyway? Somebody making some little something."

"This is disgusting."

"I don't want to play."

"Can't we change it to a *male* nurse?"

"No."

"An orderly?"

SOME WEEKS LATER

We started an exercise program and are moving about more. Eighteen women have an amazing number of limbs. There are problems of collision and entanglement, especially for me, the tallest. Somebody else is walking around with my pedicure. Eighteen women take an incredibly long time to get ready for bed, and at night, Flavia, who sleeps at my feet, grinds her teeth on her bite plate. Today, though, I cheered everyone up by pretending to be a barmaid—taking orders and serving imaginary drinks. More discussion as we sipped our slings, toddies, and shrubs.

"I don't ask much of a man, but there must be something more variegated than this."

"He's a drip."

"His life is a mess and he had no right to involve us in it."

"Get serious. We came here on our own thirty-six feet."

"But remain under duress."

"Reread your Millstonecraft and De Beauwoolf. Duress is no one-way street."

"Well, it ain't the Boulevard of Dreams."

"All I know is, this situation is his fault and I'm not leaving here till he does something about it."

SUMMER

Over the past months, impatience has driven us to accumulate some power, mostly by mail order. Flavia has obtained, under a false name, membership in the St. Vincent Ferrer Boys' Club, from a membership mill in Alabama. Rufa has gained possession of a quantity of information, which she carries in a briefcase of quality leather. Narcissa has become adept at power yoga and sits cross-legged three hours a day, intoning, "I won't knuckle under to the marketing arm." Chloe is making a knife. I am a matriculant in a correspondence school and have learned to draw pie graphs with the largest wedge labeled Fossil Fools. I'm not sure we're getting this stuff right.

Today Rufa took a paper out of her briefcase and said, "I'm going to work on my peach." Narcissa put one arm around her protectively and said, "She means her *speech*. You mean your *speech,* don't you, honey."

LATE SUMMER

The lack of food is, to me, one of the most unfortunate features of

Just as I was starting to write, an astonishing thing happened. I was staring up at the only window, which is high in the wall opposite the door and covered with a stout latticework of nylon rope. Through the window I could see patches of bright green against a background of gray cement that I know to be the west façade of the Port Authority building. From here, the gray has a sparse, dry quality, devoid of physical presence, and I was seized by the inexplicable remoteness of life in confinement. Then I noticed that the patches of green were moving, falling. They looked like hunks of lawn or artificial turf. Divots! That can mean only one thing: he lives directly above us and is none other than the Midnight Ambler, the international outlaw who disdainfully terrorizes women by flaunting his preference for a form of miniature golf played on a mined course, roaming the dark streets with his diminutive putter in search of an all-night game.

We decided to confront him with what we know. We composed the letter collectively:

"We know who you are," I began. "You are the man known as the Midnight Ambler, long sought by the Geneva police on charges of failure to attend a compulsory educational film on the estrogen cycle."

"We know you are the enemy of women everywhere, and so we are no longer at the mercy of your every move—"

"Or should we say your every failure to move. Love us or leave us, we could care less. Your behavior is wrong."

"Grievously wrong."

"More wrong than you'll ever know."

"Wrong and then some."

"We are leaving. We have the power to do that now, because we have come to care less about you than you care about us—"

"If that is possible."

"If it is not possible, we have the power anyway. Until we get it together to leave, we demand regular meals. We also demand free beer and soda, and all other drinks at half price."

Some of the women see our ultimatum as a ploy and hope it will penetrate his heart. The rest study the rope latticework at the window and practice neck craning in an effort to work out some means of escape.

We all show signs of nervousness. Earlier, Flavia's bite plate fell onto the floor with a tiny *click* and we stampeded for forty-five minutes.

THE NEXT MORNING

When we awoke, the bonbon services were filled with scrambled eggs. At each place was a demitasse of hot coffee. Under each cup was a letter, folded many times. The letters were all handwritten but in content identical:

Darling: I have been wrong. I offer no excuses for my crimes, but try to understand. I was a middle child. I was a planned child; and because I was planned, I thought I must seek a perfection that I now realize is hateful, for it leaves others with nothing to forgive, which is too little, or everything to forgive, which is too much. I was arrested for peeping at the age of six. Of the rest of my career, you know the essentials. I am overtired. The point is, I have changed. Last year, I sought out eighteen of you at random, in the hope that

one or two of you might work out. I have been watching you
through a hole in the floor of my room. This has been a healing
experience for me. You have all worked out. You have not hurt me,
and until now you have asked for nothing in return. I have fallen in
love with you. I am prepared to trust you. I am prepared to give up
my freedom, for freedom is an idea so nearly perfect that the only
thing left to do is renounce it. I have ordered mother-of-pearl wain-
scoting for your room, and for the bath a Steri-Matron, which dries
the hands in antiseptic waves of ultraviolet light and electrically
generated hot air. I have had eighteen canvas carry-alls printed up
with my photograph on them, and I wish to present one to each of
you personally, tonight at midnight, when the silk-screening is dry.
At that time I shall ask you to marry me and remain here so that I
can worship you forever. Truly I am a worshiper of women. Could I
be otherwise with such an anguished past?

XXXXXX
XXXXXX
XXXXXX

The Midnight Ambler.

Some of the younger ones cried. But the discussion was brief:
"It's not enough. What he's offering."
"Do we *have* to hold out for enough?"
"I believe he loves me. But he took too long."
"Too long for what?"
"Still, a lot of that time he was writing out these letters."
"I kind of empathize. Is that crazy?"
We agreed: everybody's got to go.

THAT AFTERNOON

We have been talking over the problem of the favorite. We
know, from our reading in the literature of harems, that there
is always a favorite. We also know, from our reading in the
literature of favoritism, that the favorite is not always the best.

That she may have advanced herself by perfidy, pregnancy, or willingness to take on administrative tasks. That even when she is the best, she will, at the whim of the favorer, be supplanted by a new favorite, who may have advanced herself by currying, cowrie-shell amulets, or willingness to transcend mere administrative tasks. We know that the system can accommodate only one favorite at a time. We know that the favorite will high-hat the others, and that the others will wish to blow the favorite to kingdom come.

We are determined that if we stay—which we won't—there must be no favorites.

THAT EVENING

It is almost time to put away this journal. I have attempted to explore here the dualities in my own nature, which, when I look into the mirror, I see even in my face: the upper half all eyes and nose, the lower all mouth and chin. The eyes and nose of an ordinary woman, the mouth and chin of a favorite.

LATER

We found that we could lift the smallest of us up to the window and hold her by her ankles while she cut the ropes with Chloe's knife. By this time it was midnight. In the dark room, women were raised to the window, one by one. I could hear the soft rending of blue chiffon as they dropped to the street below. I, the tallest, was left for last. The others tied the bits of rope together and tossed one end back to me through the window. I took it. I wanted to see the Midnight Ambler.

I must have been standing there for a few minutes, barely hearing the whispered instructions from outside, when a fold of satin gleamed in the room: the Ambler. He was all in white, and his looks were definitely not a disappointment—a good build dominated by a single head. In one hand he carried a silver putter.

"What do you want?" I asked, trembling.

"It's you who want," he said. "I watched the escape through my floor. You waited."

"I wanted to find out what you want."

"Polygamy is on the way out," he said, "and not only among the masses. Even members of the National Security Council now content themselves with one wife. Someone must take up the slack. This is the moment I have been waiting for. It coincides with some change in myself. I love all of you. Persuade them to stay. You can do it. They respect you, you're cultivated, you're tall. What do I want? Call it an extended family. An ordinary man and ordinary women, together going about their daily tasks—shutting the kitchen door, leaving footprints up and down the hall, listening to the cockerel crow, living an ordinary life."

"What do you know of ordinary life?" I said. "Do you know the difference between an infant and a newborn baby? What are the three hidden signs of charm and personality in a spouse? In a society not dependent on subsistence production and in which the inside of a gal's purse is not considered an index of character, how do you decide which wife will be the favorite?"

"I don't want to hurt anybody."

"Maybe you should favor Flavia. She's O.K.—almost a virgin and not quite a dunce. Or Narcissa—not quite ugly and almost sane. Or Chloe—almost decent and not quite dead."

"Or you," he said. His cologne was subtle and deranging.

"It's hard to know," I said, "whether to ruin everything just to satisfy one's own erotic curiosity."

"Ruin?" he said. "Ruin is par for the course."

I wasn't ready for this. I took the rope and, struggling, began to climb. I felt him moving quickly toward me, and then I felt a rung beneath my foot. I looked down: the silver putter.

"Thank you," I said.

"You must love freedom," he said.

"Some of it."

I settled the arch of my foot firmly on the putter and pushed myself up and through the window. What seemed at that moment like forever turned out to be a relatively long time.

Curb Carter Policy Discord Effort Threat

WASHINGTON, OCT. 11—In a surprise move, a major spokesman announced yesterday that a flurry of moves has forestalled deferment of the Administration's controversial hundred-pronged strategy. The nine-page indictment provides a minimum of new details about the alleged sharp apprehensions now being voiced in key areas. As holiday traffic flowed into and out of the nation's cities, President Carter acknowledged in a telephone interview that there is "cause for some optimism." But Senate conferees quickly vowed to urge the challenging of this view as over-optimistic.

In a shocking about-face, it was confirmed that the package will serve as the basis for mounting pressures. However, no target date has been set for the fueling of speculations.

In an unexpected development, it is expected that fresh pleas will be issued for a brightened outlook. "Sharply higher deficits will rise in the long run," said a senior expert. Token collection of heavy weapons has been reported near the austerity programs, where a newly minted spirit of fairness has caused anticipated losses.

The focal point of this change of focus is the Administration's broad-gauge diplomatic push. According to officials in the vogue for docu-dramas, these figures indicate that a shrinking supply of farmland, swept by strong emotional tides and waves of public resentment, is considering another round of direct contacts with the globe's expanding circle of treelessness. However, flagrant lobbying, emerging violations, and tenacious complicating factors have now knocked the expected bloodbath into an increasingly powerful cocked hat, say sources. Meanwhile, cracks in the alliance have erupted, linking harsh inroads with a lagging industrial base.

Last week, the coalition warned that 152 recommendations would be submitted, cutting deeply into the support for renewed wrangling. But such policies have long irked the delegates, and the fear now is that they will sound a death knell to the Constitution by muting their quarrels or adding that there are still elements to be ironed out.

Embattled leaders have long lengthened the rift by using such strategies as sidedown, slowmate, staletracking, and stiffening. Now aides predict a downgrading and stymying of routine foreign cutoffs, unless the nuclear family can be bailed out of this legal vacuum. Dr. Bourne reasserted his innocence of any wrongdoing.

The transitional Government will close for defusing next week, without having resolved core conflicts or posed the uneasy questions that might assuage local hard-liners. However, an authorized biography is likely to continue for months, possibly even years, to come. Not all styles in all sizes.

Continued on Page D6, Column 1

Kemp, Dent in Reagan Plans

A few hours after George Steinbrenner vowed that the New York Yankees would not trade Bucky Dent, the Yankees traded Dent to the Republicans for Jack Kemp.

The trade was announced at a press conference at Yankee Stadium just after a doubleheader between the two teams, in which the Yankees won the first game, $560,000 to $240,500. The Reagan team then shut out New York, $98.3 billion to 0, with a murderous tax bill in the top of the ninth.

Later, in the locker room, Dent was asked about his new position. He will represent upstate New York in the U.S. House of Representatives. "I'm comfortable with it," he said. "I haven't been all that happy with the Yankees recently. Mr. Steinbrenner was constantly on my back about fiscal this and earnings that, and he told me my work on last year's annual report wasn't thought very highly of in the front office. At one point he tried to make me sell individual pizzas during games—something to do with revenue. And then a few months ago he declared a three-for-one split—me, Nettles, and Smalley having to take turns going down to Wall Street to sit around the Stock Exchange and see if anybody would give us some money. Now at least Mr. Reagan has made it clear that all he wants me to do is play ball."

"So what!" Steinbrenner steamed when Dent's remarks were read to him as he sought a limousine.

Reportedly, the idea for a trade came from the White House Office of Player Personnel, the Bechtel Group, which released this statement: "Jack Kemp is a very fine young man, and the Reagan organization is very sorry to see him leave Washington. We all have the greatest respect for his lovely family. He should be grateful for all that Ronald Reagan has done for him."

At an impromptu briefing on the White House helicopter pad, Reagan waved, smiled, and said, "I sensed Jack wasn't happy, because he couldn't keep his mind on the gate receipts. He kept nagging day in and day out about spending what-all and the other thing, supply, and he frankly just made a nuisance. It was time to cut the guy loose. He'll be better off in a situation where I won't always be having to have to prove I'm sane."

However, Kemp's spokesman, talent agent Bob Haldeman, said, "Jack loves his teammates in the Capitol, but he is a sincere idealist who actually believes that George Steinbrenner is a man of unswerving principle—unlike some other people who Jack has too much integrity to comment on."

Invited to reply to this by a TV newscaster waiting at Andrews Air Force Base, Reagan chuckled and burst out spontaneously, "You know, I'd love to go back into show business. It would be fun to do that vaudeville routine where you take a Jack-in-the box and hit it with a hammer. But seriously. Jack Kemp sure in Hades didn't turn out to be a team player, which is how I never thought in the first place. Where is the sportsmanship that his wonderful parents instilled? Who does he think he is, as he seems to think?"

Flagged down on a California freeway, former Yankee manager Billy Martin was asked for his opinion of the trade. While
explaining carefully that Steinbrenner needed to be taken
down a peg or two, Martin drove away.

A source close to a companion of Reggie Jackson's main-
tained guardedly that "Reggie is keeping a positive mental atti-
tude at all times."

Steinbrenner is rumored to have really hit the ceiling on
hearing this.

Later in the day, the cause of Steinbrenner's ire was divulged
when he chewed out an ebullient Reagan in a limo driven by
an undercover reporter. Steinbrenner had begun the negotia-
tions months ago, when the Reagan organization was trying to
unload David Stockman. At the last minute, Reagan jawboned
Steinbrenner into taking Kemp off his hands as the precondi-
tion for a Stockman deal. Now the Yankees have had to arrange to sell Kemp to M-G-M–United Artists and buy Stockman outright for an undisclosed sum of cash.

Stockman's old position, Director of the Office of Manage-
ment and Budget, will be held down by a callboy.

After hearing this news from his representative, West Coast
super-agent Ham Jordan, Stockman telephoned a reporter at
home and confided, "It's tremendous news, just tremendous—
a tremendous break for me. Ever since I was a little baby, I've
wanted a position on the New York Yankees, with all the joy
in economic performance that makes it worthwhile. An impossible dream, but then—you know me! I have a way of getting
myself into situations that are way over my head and then
flagellating myself for failing to overcome the tremendous
odds. I don't know—maybe that's even what I'm doing right
now. Setting myself up for failure. O.K.! Let's say I'm asking
for trouble, it's probably hopeless, but it's the chance of a life-

time—to be with a winner. What an exciting prospect! The Reagan thing, you know, began to change tremendously once it started to not work out. There is athlete's foot on the Presidency. It is growing. It compounds itself daily, like interest. It's a phenomenal—a giant fungus! How do we keep it off us? For all I know, maybe the whole world, even the Yankees, is doomed necessarily to be this type of uncontrollable—these things of this nature, and the like, which allow no one to function within them as a rational shortstop. What did I just say? Are you writing this down?"

Reached for a reaction in what he described as "the middle of the night," Reagan said laughingly, "If that's his interpretation, all I can say is he's as equally as entitled to it as I am. Very frankly, he has always had a loose rotator cuff. Like the rest of the country, it is very sad for his family and we have great sympathy. Bucky Dent—now there is a very popular young man with our American population. As far as Jack Kemp, it's not my job to make trades for the Yankees, but they bought a pig in a poke there, and they have nothing but our compassion."

Kemp's personal manager, Jerry Ford, said, "Jack Kemp can play hardball with the best of them. But he has a frail ego like all professional egomaniacs. And this career instability at this point is affecting his athletic condition."

Reagan's phone was off the hook by then, but his aide Lyn Nofziger, "psychiatrist to the stars," commented, "I knew Jack Kemp wouldn't last five minutes in a business such as the New York Yankees."

The Reagan History of the United States

[President] McKinley gave Rowan a letter to be
delivered to Garcia; Rowan took the letter and did
not ask, "Where is he at?" ... It is not booklearning
young men need, nor instruction about this and
that, but a stiffening of the vertebrae which will
cause them to be loyal to a trust, to act promptly,
concentrate their energies; do the thing—
"carry a message to Garcia!"
... We have recently been hearing much maudlin
sympathy for the "down-trodden denizen of the
sweat-shop" and the "homeless wanderer searching
for honest employment," and with it all go many
hard words for the men in power....
In our pitying, let us drop a tear, too, for the men
who are striving to carry on a great enterprise whose
working hours are not limited by the whistle, and
whose hair is fast turning white through the struggle
to hold in line dowdy indifference....
My heart goes out to the man ... who, when given a
letter for Garcia, quietly takes the missive, without
asking any idiotic questions, and with no lurking
intention of chucking it into the nearest sewer, or of
doing aught else but deliver it, never gets "laid-off,"
nor has to go on a strike for higher wages.
Civilization is one long anxious search
for just such individuals.
—Elbert Hubbard, "A Message to Garcia," 1899

*Worried and embarrassed officials of a YMCA in Washington,
D.C., confirmed that a man who penetrated the Y's security
system late one night, entering a top-floor room through a win-*

dow and sitting on a resident's bed to talk for about fifteen minutes, was President Ronald Reagan.

The YMCA resident, an unemployed librarian named Manuel Garcia, stated, "He shook me awake and read me this sort of bedtime story. He said it contained a 'message' that would 'promote backbone, eliminating pessimism and fear.' Fortunately, while he was reading; my vertebrae did stiffen to the degree that I was able to edge slowly toward the door."

President Reagan told reporters that he had been "disappointed" when Mr. Garcia voiced a need to go down the hall to bum a cigarette and never returned. "I was trying to bring the lessons of American history to the unemployed. Nowadays, you know, if you want something done, you have to do it yourself. Oh, well—what can you expect from someone who the incredible filth they live in? You wouldn't believe the room. All over the floor—when you step down from the windowsill, it's literally knee-deep in bills, letters from collection agencies, repo notices, foreclosure documents, all just chucked on the floor like a sewer. To put one foot in there, I had to swallow very hard."

The President said that the story he had read aloud while perched at the foot of Mr. Garcia's bed was a fable about "the general, vague drift of what has happened to our country's ideals. Of course," he continued, "I was influenced in getting the concept and the writing style by our magnificent oil-company copywriters. And we have had some other pretty good utopian literature, too, which I had the opportunity to leaf through in the White House collection, thanks to so many of our fine historical writers of the past, whose ideas belong to us all today. I take full responsibility for their great words inserted alongside with my own."

He then distributed to reporters copies of his story.

Once upon a time, there was a Foolish Village and a Wise Village. The Foolish Villagers were a naive people who believed they could wish away their problems by electing a Council of Fools, which was inadequate to the complexities of government, being merely citizens who had chosen to meddle in council affairs. The villagers, many in bikinis, rode to work on colorful bicycles, heedless of the potential painful muscle infirmities. "Let us work hard today," they said, "and spend what we have earned tomorrow," ignoring one or two sober, level heads who predicted that the convoy of fools might wobble on the roadbed of economic inertia.

Youth no longer stunted and starved; age no longer harried by avarice; the child at play with the tiger; the man with the muck-rake drinking in the glory of the stars! Foul things fled, fierce things tame; discord turned to harmony!

Believing in all that, the Foolish Villagers became preoccupied with hedonistic woolgathering about the present and future. Most allowed their interest in television to dwindle, and swarmed instead to argument-provoking public debates and fetish parlors. Still others hunkered mindlessly over their vegetable gardens, where unauthorized sex proliferated, or lay reading idly beneath frail solar-heating panels that dotted the rooftops where they had been hastily flung up in the expectation of "something for nothing."

Adultery, assassination, poisoning, and other crimes of the like infernal nature, were taught as lawful, and even as virtuous actions. Men were set upon each other, like a company of hellhounds to worry, rend and destroy.

When, under discreet cover of darkness, concerned oil-company representatives converged on the area, the brass fittings on their efficient portfolios burnished by moonlight, the village was ill equipped to comply with their suggestions.

Human nature goes not straight forward but by excessive action and reaction in an undulated course.

Unable, or unwilling, to change course, the village tumbled

into receivership. The only remaining business was a dingy waxworks arcade, where morose children, many in tattered bikinis, paid a penny to file past amateurishly modeled figurines of their parents, whose legacy to the new generation was only a hollow smile.

The Wise Village, however, adopted the long-term strategy needed to forestall trouble: success.

Giant miraculous Labor was felling the forests, and turning the glebe, and whirling the spinning jennies, and putting down its thoughts in words and deeds; the spires of an hundred thousand schoolhouses pointed to the skies; the fires of truth and self-sacrifice glowed in many more thousand breasts; the noblest aspirations were ascending from millions of noble souls.

A Coalition of Alarmed Fathers, democratically appointed on the basis of merit, had responded decisively to the incentives offered by several major enterprises in which they were stockholders, and the Wise Village was flooded with petroleum products, to the extent that some stores had to close for inventory. Heavy industries—such as psychiatry and inventory-taking—began to blossom, turning the village into a hub of cosmopolitanism visited by the duly nominated, exotically garbed delegates of various juntas and well-wishing corporations from South of the Border, the Land of the Rising Sun, and the Back of Beyond.

Penalties, temporal and eternal; splendour, pomp, and honour; united to terrify, to dazzle, to awe and to flatter the human mind.

Dressed in handsome frontier-style garments scarcely distinguishable from the finest clothing, and uninhibited by shortsighted utilitarian carping about the effects of ornamental garters upon the blood circulation of the women, the villagers drove roomy automobiles to and from the exciting inventory parlors that gave texture and variety to the naturally flat cement landscape, or spontaneously entertained themselves by leafing through the brightly illustrated booklets of Rules and Regulations dispensed free to all by television repairmen.

Was there, then, no way of commanding the services of the mighty wealth-producing principle of consolidated capital without bowing down to a plutocracy like that of Carthage? As soon as men began to ask themselves this question, they found the answer ready for them.

Gold!

The news rapidly spread, and there was soon a large number of men on the spot, some of whom obtained several pounds per day, at the start. The gulch had been well dug up for the large lumps, but there was still great wealth in the earth and sand, and several operators only waited for the wet season to work it in a systematic manner. Secure in possessing the "Open Sesamé" to the exhaustless treasury under their feet, they gave free rein to every whim or impulse which could possibly be gratified.

A vigorous series of sporadic wars was initiated against the Foolish Village, as a means of acquiring raw materials to manufacture more guns. The young men, having demonstrated their bravery, had no need to "prove" their masculinity by deflorations of young girls, and within a decade a Council of Wise Virgins was authorized to sit with the Coalition of Alarmed Fathers, in an advisory capacity. The President of the Coalition looked about him in satisfaction. With the money markets under control, the ax falling regularly upon the necks of criminals, and the Foolish Village duly subdued and annexed under the provisions of an Extemporaneous Amendment, there appeared to remain no irrational force to wreck his accomplishments.

But a Malefactor, accused of *Witchcraft* as well as *Murder*, and Executed in this place more than Forty Years ago, did then give Notice, of, *An Horrible PLOT against the Country by* WITCHCRAFT, *and a Foundation of* WITCHCRAFT *then Laid, which if it were not seasonably Discovered, would probably Blow up, and pull down all the Churches in the country.* An Army of *Devils* horribly broke in upon the place which is the *Center:* and the Houses of the Good People there, fill'd with the doleful Shrieks of their Children and Servants.

Even as the President sternly pointed his finger at the Focus of Evil, his House began to emit conflicting rhetorical signals, and sprang a series of *Malicious* LEAKS.

Garcia was somewhere in the mountain fastnesses of Cuba—no one knew where. No mail or telegraph message could reach him. The President must secure his co-operation, and quickly.

> —written with HENRY GEORGE,
> TIMOTHY DWIGHT, MARGARET
> FULLER, PARKE GODWIN, JOHN
> TAYLOR, EDWARD BELLAMY, BAYARD
> TAYLOR, COTTON MATHER, and
> ELBERT HUBBARD

Pac Hits Fan

In the wake of the elections, a force to be reckoned with has petered out into an ill wind. The richest and hitherto most dreaded of the Political Action Committees, the National Team for Promoting Itself and a Conservative Congress (NTPICC), aims to guide public debate into a vortex of underlying negativity in such a way that the overriding importance of NTPICC is revealed. During the campaign, NTPICC spent $40 million to spread 40 rumors, to direct-mail 400 outright lies, to place 4,000 unflattering advertisements, and to deliver 40,000 demagogic salvos, generating a 40 percent higher fear factor. However, only three candidates targeted by NTPICC were defeated: Representative Paul J. Mangle (D-Mich.), Senator Joseph P. Skorfones (R-Ill.), and Representative Dominic Egregio (D-N.Y.). Each had received a 50 percent rating from the Americans for Democratic Action and a 50 percent rating from the American Conservative Union, as NTPICC's ads and press releases repeatedly pointed out in denouncing the three as "wishy-washy" by comparison with NTPICC's own decisive tornado of ads and press releases.

In Tennessee, where Republican Senator Winton K. Nullings was beaten in his bid for a fifth term, NTPICC circulated a cropped photo purporting to show his Democratic opponent, Representative Maurice B. Spran, all alone. But Spran's staff indignantly released the original, showing a number of active, involved staff members, cute interns, and ABSCAM informants in the picture. The fine points of the photographic fraud were not lost on the voters, despite their *perception* of what *might* have been true had the truth lain somewhere.

In an attempt to defeat Democrat Joseph F. X. Scullery, Jr., who was running for a Massachusetts Congressional seat, NTPICC aired 400,000 TV spots featuring pirated footage of a National Endowment for the Arts–funded dance troupe, dressed in ecclesiastical garb and miming the sixteenth-century papal ban on opera while a voice-over charged that Mr. Scullery was dodging the issue of federally subsidized opera as a form of government-imposed birth control. Mr. Scullery remained unaware of the commercials, but even if he had not, he would have *appeared* to remain unaware of them.

Thousands of schoolchildren were hired by New Jersey NTPICC to deliver complimentary frozen ducks to undecided households. But the bribery tactic backfired on incumbent Republican Congressman Phil ("Pete") Musser, who spent the rest of the campaign denying that he had ever said the freeze was a canard. And in Florida, Republican Congresswoman Estelle Hexler never recovered from her 40-point drop in the polls when her elderly constituents were deluged with NTPICC mailings of "ballot cards" asking whether they favored a constitutional amendment to mandate that mandatory prayers be printed on Social Security checks in place of payable dollar amounts. In both cases, the facts of the matter were difficult to establish in the absence of a certainty that the matter existed, and exit polls showed a voter failure to receive this or that *impression*.

NTPICC may have been weakened by the recently published book *A Pac with the Devil,* by the late Percy Prang, which asserts that NTPICC's leader, Yancy Lang, who has vigorously supported the death penalty, has himself been dead for four years. NTPICC's power may also be eroded by a newly formed anti-action-committee action committee, Bust Action Committees with Plain-Ass Common Sense (BACPACS), which is already planning a defense of Senator Sam Spofford (D-Va.) two years from now. Spofford is sure to be singled out by NTPICC, because it is angered by the way his frequent, popular appearances on D.C.-area TV and radio talk shows deplete the air time available for NTPICC to single him out.

NTPICC has already announced that most of its resources for the next election will go into targeting five Democratic and five Republican members of the House: John Peter Telly (D-Conn.), Gary G. McGreen (D-Ore.), Martha Fortfield Garglan (D-Pa.), Paul J. Kowlicki (D-Minn.), Bill Bobbin, Jr. (D-Vt.), Hamilton R. Schneehart (R-Calif.), Mengel A. Puppe (R-Ga.), Earl B. Ninick (R-Okla.), John O. Calf (R-Nev.), and Ermeto P. Invigorita (R-N.J.). NTPICC argues that these people are "deadwood," since their votes in the House cancel each other out. This theory may be irrefutable, but if it can be *seen* as speckled with flaws, NTPICC itself might be on the spot.

The Sacred Front

> The day was as fine and the scene was as fair at
> Newmarch as the party was numerous and various;
> ... I don't know why—it was a sense instinctive
> and unreasoned, but ... I was just conscious,
> vaguely, of being on the track of a law, a law that
> would fit, that would strike me as governing the
> delicate phenomena—delicate though so marked—
> that my imagination found itself playing with.
> —Henry James, *The Sacred Fount*

> Anyone with an eye and an ear for the nuances of a
> new sensibility should be able to detect the telltale
> signs of the new cold war culture.
> —Andrew Kopkind, "The Return of Cold War
> Liberalism," *The Nation,* April 23, 1983

1.

As Gilbert Long strode vigorously toward me on the station
platform, he struck me as so uncharacteristically alive that I
concluded he must be having a liberating sex experience with
someone. For more than a decade we had met at least semi-
annually, at Newmarch, where we were both again now bound
and where his quotidian plodding dullness had been bearable
only in that it was essential—for what was Newmarch if not a
sense of coalition kept up by everyone's being so conscious that
they were not just tolerant but, at the minimum, liberal?
Which is not to say that if one was at Newmarch, Newmarch
hadn't its reasons, beyond proving that it could suffer a bore or
two, a couple of bleached-out spots in the social fabric. Among
its reasons was that the whole fine enterprise required a certain

number of warm bodies. Of these I had judged Long hardly the
warmest, but as we settled into adjoining seats on the train, I
thought how markedly he had evolved. On the evidence of his
progress, I might have been justified in reserving a ticket for
utopia.

His eyes, rarely seen to move in their sockets, now intently
scanned our car, but if the face he sought—his lover's?—was
there, it was obscured behind one of a sea of copies of Radosh
and Milton's new book on the Rosenberg case, though the only
"spying" for which *I* was willing to shoulder blame was my
own prying avidity to take the erotic measure of Long's im-
provement. I could scarcely defend my urge to snoop by pre-
maturely accusing him of privatism; hadn't he the right to
hoard his new relationship for a time before contributing it to
the general consciousness for analysis? Yet guiltily I couldn't
stop my eyes from following his, and he fairly caught me out:

"I'm only looking," he said, "for the other dupes and stooges
among these fellow-travelers."

The thrust showed an ironic wit of which he had hitherto
been judged incapable; this virile comedian was not the same
drab timid institution who had driven even as indulgent a
comrade as "Do Your Own Thing" Lutley to dub him "the
Great Gray Lady." With my astonished amusement egging
him on, he grew still more delightful on the subject of a film
he had seen—just a television miniseries, *The Winds of War,*
but as I recall he put across one or two very clever ideas,
couched in satiric form. Further emboldened by my good-na-
tured responsiveness, he consolidated his position by ringing
for a porter to remove me from my seat so he could "spread
out." As I was carried reluctantly down the aisle, I wondered
again about his lover, and about the passion whose effect was
so revolutionary.

2.

When we drew near our station, and passengers began gathering their luggage, Long passed me to position himself at the door and be first off the train, saying he had "a horror of mob rule." I was still laughing when, surprised by a stinging sensation on my shoulder, I looked around, up a statuesque figure, and into the stern, lovely face of a stranger.

"Traitor," she said.

That was hard—but then I was struck by something else, a familiarity that made me guess she might be soft on this particular treason.

"Do you dare snub me?" she asked. And as it dawned that she was indeed Grace Brissenden, she playfully dealt me another lash with what I saw to be the black leather horsewhip she famously carried, by reputation the one Emma Goldman had used to punish a fellow-anarchist turncoat. At Newmarch, some of us practically worshiped this dazzling accessory.

"It's only," I pleaded, "that I didn't recognize you."

"Because I was wrapped up in that book about those sp—"

"Because you're so *young!*" The year before, she had turned a manifest forty-five, but so magnificently that any sexist or agist slipping into Newmarch by mistake would have been hard put to classify Grace Brissenden other than as we did ourselves: as the most beautiful among persons in principle beautifully equal. Walking now with her from the train, I tried to pinpoint her transformation, and finally attributed it to a revitalized posture. She was taut; her spine seemed to vibrate, like an antenna receiving a signal: *There's something out there. . . . Don't be intimidated!* Now and then she inclined forward, daring whatever was "out there" to "play chicken." Her body she had wholly given over to what one might call brinksmanship. It took thirty years off her; it put her in a pony tail and a circle skirt in the 1950s.

But when I said as much, she recoiled disingenuously. "Nonsense, these faded baggy bell-bottoms from the sixties are 'retro' enough for an old woman like me. Anyway, Guy likes them."

Indeed, it was Guy Brissenden I presumed to be the source of her rejuvenation. Word of their marriage five months earlier had sent shock waves through the Newmarch group; but Grace and Guy were, if anyone was, up to taking the curse off matrimonialism. For a start, his being twenty years her junior gave the thing a redeeming unorthodoxy. And then, his black curls, his darting boyish curiosity, his eagerness to learn how the world, in practice, really worked, counterpointed the golden goddess-like mystique that made people believe Grace already knew everything. Together they were an aesthetically delectable pair, and we, after all, weren't puritans. Besides, if marriage gave *them* pleasure—well, we weren't dictators! Nor were they, it seemed, to one another; Grace told me Guy had come out to Newmarch the day before with Lady John. Catching the gleam of approval in my eye, she smiled:

"Yes, it's matrimonialism with a human face."

3.

A considerate anarchy being the prevalent mode at Newmarch—one never so much as touched on the matter of who might "own" the place, or whether "Newmarch" was the town or the house or simply the name fitted to our common idea—I made no formal greetings but went straight to my room. The same was invariably held for me, but as I opened the door, I wondered if I had been "frozen out," for on my bed, with his back to me, sat a naked old man with gray wisps of hair, muttering as if he were quite at home.

"Excuse me," I said, "but I think you're in my room."

He turned to me a fragile, wrinkled face. "*My* room, *your* room, what's the point? We have no need of boundaries or borders any longer. Aren't we all citizens of the planet earth?" He seized my suitcase and began rifling it. As I wrestled it from his feeble grasp, he selected a pair of my undershorts and put them on. "I dislike street clothes," he serenely explained. "They obscure the fundamental likeness of all citizens of the earthly planet. How many three-piece suits do you guess would survive a nuclear apocalypse?" He had got hold of my passport. "You won't be needing this now."

"Just who do you think you are?" I cried.

"Guy Brissenden, of course, but I know what you mean. What do names signify, when we all put on our shorts one leg at a time?"

He was, I suddenly saw, who he said he was, yet as altered by his tottering decrepitude as was his wife by her youthquake. Had my eyes not just then lighted on a socialist pamphlet that had tumbled from my suitcase during our struggle, I might never have located the cause. The redistribution of wealth! He had given *her* his youth. His recompense was—what? Inner peace, which he now meant to globalize, bestowing upon the rest of us earthlings his panacea for world brotherhood. Take, I urged myself, the analysis, correct as it is thus far, still farther. By analogy, mightn't Gilbert Long, former mental proletarian of our community, have according to his need expropriated *his* just portion from his lover? And wouldn't *she* then, by extrapolation, be the very one among us whose capital wit had been the most depleted?

I was all aware that outsiders might see her and poor Guy as being, by the other two, exploited. But if I found an attractive, progressive pattern in what superficially resembled a sordid survival of the fittest—well, wasn't what Newmarch had given *me* precisely that warm optimism?

4.

A chill was in the autumn air as we gathered on the patio for cocktails. I had my secret mission, but I couldn't find a fourth person, let alone a woman, who had dramatically changed. May Server was still pretty in her wraithlike way, with that hibiscus she always pathetically wore in her hair to "make an effort" and that signature expression of numb terror. Judging from Ford Obert's gestures, he was telling her for the umpteenth time the story of how his Yiddish-speaking father, an immigrant to Detroit, had named him "Ford" in the militant belief that the boy would live to oversee the UAW's capture of the means of production of automotive commodities. He told it movingly, and May was probably the only one there who found its repetition tedious; she would, under cover of her zombie manner, be fixating on some cryptic, peripheral detail, which she would hone to a morbid gem of description and later produce unnervingly at table, like a filigree dinner ring wrought from a human hair. I was fascinated by her being there yet not one of the crowd, in it yet so very "out of it"; but when I moved to join them, I was intercepted by a belligerent Lady John:

"It may be too soon to tell, but in the opinion of very many highly placed people it is not too soon to say that the time is coming when we may well have reason to fear the same kind of thing that once tore this country apart. 'Stalinist menace' may be too harsh a term in the opinion of some very indifferently placed people, but if I were you, I would consider whether the conventional wisdom is not urgently in need of being rethought."

Clearly she was inebriated. *Her* value had always lain as much in her soothing capacity to restate infinitely the obvious as in the eccentric taste for thrift-shop British couture which had given rise to the nickname "Lady." Now, stewed to the gills and babbling enigmatic prophecies, her Norman Hartnell pillbox aggressively awry, she was if anything *more* interesting. As Gilbert's Long's putative partner, she was therefore dismissable, along with May, from contention.

Mercifully, Grace Brissenden loomed before us. "Go along, darling Lady," she commanded, teetering threateningly and giving the pillbox a mock tap with Emma Goldman's horsewhip. "Do go find my husband, won't you? You're the only person here who amuses him."

In Grace's cool blue eyes lurked some obscure tactic, but I didn't ask what, so eager was I to divert her subtlety to my own design. Briefly, I told her about my theory, omitting of course any unflattering reference to poor Guy's virtual senility.

"Why, that's riveting!" she said. "Aren't you clever! I wonder who she can be? I know that in principle we've no right to assume it's not a *he*, but I don't blame you for not thinking of it. If Long wasn't 'straight' before, I'll bank on my instinct that he is now. You must let me know the minute you flush her out. I insist that you work on nothing else all weekend. I'll keep *my* eyes open too, and report back. Off you go!"

Somehow, it occurred to me, I *was* "off," but my sounding board had already vanished into the crowd. My speculation drifted to Mrs. Froome, our distinguished feminist theoretician, but she was said to have recently concluded an unhappy affair with an alcoholic chauffeur from the Soviet Embassy, and could be heard shrilling the virtues of hearth and home, as a cover for her disappointment, while her interlocutor, "Do Your Own Thing" Lutley, nodded in feigned support of her charade. There was a blond bombshell with de Dreuil, the activist actor, but she had clearly been imported from Hollywood for the occasion; they were engaged in some form of guerrilla theater, prancing about with American flags.

Lady John had by now captured poor Guy, who was maundering dreamily in his, or someone's, pajamas. Recalling that these two had come out together on the train, I wondered—as perhaps Grace mischievously had—if his maddening homilies were what had driven Lady over the brink, or if her Cassandra line was a ploy calculated to lure him back to reality by meeting her halfway.

At any rate, I had *my* little mission, and roamed about alone. Fortunately nobody paid the slightest attention to my inquisitive perambulations. There were far too many new faces, however, to suit my purpose: quite a lot of people speaking some volatile eastern European tongue that decidedly wasn't the Russian I had so often heard at Newmarch in years past, and young men in neoconservative suits whose vulnerability to nuclear damage challenged poor Guy to a long evening of proselytizing. Passing around the front of the house, I thought I saw at the bottom of the driveway a Libyan freedom fighter and a Mau-Mau being mistakenly ejected from the grounds, but before I could intervene, Grace Brissenden magically appeared at my side, saying urgently, "You must see— you must!"

The wooden deck to which she quickly led me looked out over a spacious lawn, rich with a thickening carpet of dead leaves, which rollingly descended to an herb garden surrounding a white gazebo. What happy evenings I had spent in that gazebo with Newmarch comrades, enjoying the herbs and dancing to the lilting rhythms of the Beatles' "Revolution 9"! Nowadays the herb garden gave off an odor of Paraquat, and vandals had turned the gazebo into a missile silo. In its shadow, more wraithlike than ever, stood May Server. She beckoned cajolingly to a partner, but whoever it was remained hidden on the far side.

"It *must* be Gilbert Long," said Grace. "I saw them talking together not five minutes ago."

A man's naked foot peeped out from behind the silo. "Does that look like Long's foot?"

"How ever would *I* know?" But even as she spoke, the man emerged, took May's outstretched hand, and led her back into hiding. It was poor Guy. When they failed to reappear, I concluded that they must have entered the silo by a door concealed from our line of vision.

"It's *she!*" uttered Grace in agitation. "*She's* the one!"

"Impossible," I said. "She's unchanged; she's fascinating."

"The only fascinating thing about her," said Grace, "is that she's using my husband as a screen. He's the only one too kind to see how otherwise very unfascinating she is."

"But—"

Grace wouldn't hear me out. "You're wrong," she said. "You'll see."

Dismissively, I turned away from the vista to face the house, whereupon I perceived through a window an unsettling tableau. Ford Obert and Lady John, in a far corner of the room, their heads cocked and eyes narrowed, judgmentally regarded what I at first took to be my own person. In the next instant, however, I understood that what they appraised from so objective a distance must be the big picture between the windows in the Newmarch gallery.

5.

As Grace and I entered the gallery, Gilbert Long, previously hidden from my view by an enormous unpacked crate of new acquisitions, was talking rapidly, with elegant gestures toward the older cultural icon at issue. I just failed to catch his concluding words, but the other two keenly met my eye as if to say, "Now, *here's* a fellow qualified to mediate the terms of discourse."

"What do you think of it?" Grace asked me disarmingly.

Between the windows, where it had always been, was a poster, framed in Plexiglas, some five or six feet in height, of a stylized male figure dressed from head to toe in black and wearing a black mask; the usual thing.

"Well," I said, "it's a symbol of the black man's struggle, isn't it?—I mean, all black people's struggle—to retain their ethnic identity while, on the other hand, having inescapably a consciousness that their color is a barrier—a mask, as it were—between them and their full acceptance as individuals by the white oppressor."

"I'm sure we can all agree upon *that,*" said Grace firmly, as the other three drew near. "But from *you* we expect an opinion—oh, farther out."

"Well," I went on, "you could say too that it's gay rights. In fact, wasn't there something of the kind on the cover of Burroughs' last book?"

"Why," spluttered Lady John, "Tarzan was *never*—"

Obert broke in smoothly. "I daresay it's less parochial than *that*—sympathetic though I may be to the plight of our sado-masochistic brothers and sisters."

"Well," I said, "I wouldn't put that down as a marginal concern, but I do see what you mean. I mean, the image does cry out to take in everyone."

"And that's exactly what your critique hasn't yet confronted," said Obert. "The assertion of raw monolithic all-consuming power."

I fancied that Lady John glanced for approval at Gilbert Long before she spoke. "It's totalitarian!"

"But don't you see?" I said. "The total, audaciously utter *blackness* of it—well, doesn't that inevitably imply—doesn't it compel you to imagine—its opposite?"

"You're saying that when we look at black, we should see white?" Grace smilingly prompted.

"Not only that we should—that we *do!* It's a proven law of optics. And when," I brought out triumphantly, "you sense the hidden light and allow it to flood your consciousness—well, it's astoundingly beautiful!"

"It's *horrible*," came a penetrating whisper. May Server had crept silently into the gallery during my interrogation.

"It's *about* horror, my dear," said Obert. "There I quite agree with you, whatever our well-meaning, generous-minded, light-flooded friend here may say. But that isn't quite the same thing as its being in and of itself a horror. Some of us find it a quite effectively unsentimentalized portrait of evil."

"In and of itself it's horrible," she quietly insisted, trembling. "It reminds me of the waiters' uniforms in the Sheraton coffee shop in El Salvador."

"Shouldn't we go in?" murmured Lady John ambiguously.

"Perhaps," continued Obert, "I haven't made my meaning—"

"It hasn't *got* any meaning." Now all but inaudible, May's quavering voice had somehow the effect of an anesthetizing shriek. "It's the enigma that *is* the horror. The never knowing . . . the Black Maria rounding the corner . . . the *noche de muerte* . . . the asphalt freeway, the blacking-out behind the wheel . . . the repellent swishing noise of nuns' habits brushing against army boots . . . the final annihilating nightmare of realizing that even this emblematic fugue means nothing, nothing, noth—" Outside, a champagne cork popped, and she mouthed a soundless scream and dived for cover under a coffee table.

While the others tried to lure her out, I was led aside by Grace, who said, "How do you answer her? By proposing that this—this *thing* is humanism with a fascist face?"

I couldn't tell if she was baiting me. But as she leaned over me, she seemed on the very brink of attack; I flinched, and she drew back as if satisfied.

"Darling," she said, "why don't you just concentrate on

who's sleeping with whom, and whether enough of them are blacks, and leave the rest of us, who aren't, after all, so tender and sensitive as you, to grapple with the big crude clumsy guns of international issues and practicalities."

She was charming. Why, then, did I feel dizzy, as if her charm had an ideological spin? Was something the matter at Newmarch? The only thing I was sure of was that this was no time for bothering to refute May Server's self-dramatizing drivel. Was it I who had, in my estimate of May, so thoroughly changed? Or had *she*—her mind ransacked for the greater glory of Gilbert Long's? Or had recent history simply rendered her worse than irrelevant? Poor May—in any case, her hibiscus had wilted.

6.

All unawares, I too had been rendered decidedly "out of it." Having in my ruminations taken a time to dress, I entered the dining room late and was almost palpably struck by a crowd who had humiliatingly neglected to inform me that the evening's party was a festive "theme" masquerade. Seating myself inconspicuously at the end of the table, I tried to make out the controlling motif. Ford Obert had greased his hair and shadowed his jowls in simulation of Senator Joseph McCarthy; de Dreuil, in a false mustache, adroitly mimed Dean Acheson; awash in a red silk cape and topped by a matching biretta, "Do Your Own Thing" Lutley was the cosmopolitan Bishop Fulton J. Sheen; and Gilbert Long, with a slide rule in his breast pocket, was passing out cigars and announcing that he was "the proud father of the H-bomb," Edward Teller. Most of the women must have been writhing in competitive pique, for Mrs. Froome was only the most accurate of any number of Hedda Hoppers with hats and lists of show-business subversives. Lady John, typically vague and overworking a small vocabulary of props, flourished a snifter of brandy and one of the H-bomb cigars— connoting, I guessed, Churchill. Only Grace, to my right, puzzled me: impeccably mannish in *le smoking,* she mysteriously resembled—yet how *could* she?—John Foster Dulles.

And what then *was* the theme? If it was "The Fifties," why did the Harvard professor across from me keep thrusting his forefinger at me and shouting "Ich bin ein Berliner"? And why then hadn't anyone come as Jerry Lee Lewis or Elvis or Betty "Shoop Shoop" Everett? Or Jack Paar, or Stalin? Or Marilyn, or Kinsey? Or Kukla, Fran, and Ollie, or Ethel and Julius?

Poor Guy and May straggled in last, and I felt a surge of sympathy; they too were in the dark. Guy had only changed into a fresh pair of my shorts; as he sat down on the other side of Grace, she tenderly tucked around his bare shoulders a radiation-resistant Lurex shawl. May, across from him, had merely traded her hibiscus for a fresh one—perhaps, if Grace's hypothesis was correct, sent up to her by Gilbert Long like a prom corsage; but then wouldn't her lover have plotted for her a costume that might with his covertly correspond? Instead it was poor May and poor Guy who corresponded all too obviously.

Yet I couldn't think it through to illumination, not with everyone at the table trying so agreeably, so volubly to stay "in character." Indeed, as the huge dim hall echoed with *coups de théâtre*—strident denunciations of "terrorism" and calls for "deterrence"—I felt that thought was an unwelcome guest, and that a pretty idea which happened to infiltrate the conversation might find such a reception as is awarded that comic-strip boogeyman the "KGB agent" booted out the door and onto a plane back to Moscow.

I cannot convey my happiness as, blowing desperately on the embers of our mutual consciousness, I felt there then reassuringly glow in me anew the incendiary compact by which we none of us need remind the others who we "really" were or discredit by explicitness our unfazable, indestructible harmony of purpose. And as if on cue, loudspeakers began to emit those squawks I knew were preparatory to the stereophonic musical accompaniment that always enhanced dinner at Newmarch by inducing rapt submission to the common hallucinatory spell. As the first waves of sound swept over us, silencing the dreadful talk, I could not but reflect on the power of this sublime art to persuade me that we all vibrated to the same tune, that together we sought to quench a thirst for an ideal of perfection. It was on this pitch that I should have liked to leave them all, but alas!—a developing tide in the music was now pulling me, by means of a melody deviously banal, into a mainstream of orchestral bullying.

I turned to Grace. "What *is* this—this thing?"

She laughed. "The music from *Victory at Sea!*"

7.

Later that night, I found myself pacing restlessly alone through the sitting rooms. Dinner had terminated in stasis, the party having gone straight to bed instead of evolving, in the old manner, toward caucuses for the exercise of perdurable debates. The whole place now had the air of a once busy shop on whose plate-glass window was pasted the forbidding sign "SOLD OUT."

I fiercely desired to smoke, but could find no one to smoke with. Out of habit, I strolled unthinking down to the gazebo, and experienced the awful jolt of its being now a missile silo; but remembering that I had conjectured some entry on the far side, I went around and indeed saw set in the hillside a hatch door, ajar, through which was visible none other than poor Guy. I settled on him gratefully as a suitable companion with whom to smoke; his state of consciousness already profoundly altered, he wouldn't much encroach on my supply. Besides, I wished to convey my kindly feelings—to signal that, in my detections, *I* didn't mean to encroach on whatever pleasures he and May Server had privately stashed.

He looked more wizened than ever, hunched at a desk, engaged with paper and colored pencils in some sort of drawing. Seeing me, he hastened to cover his work with a manila envelope.

"Oh, I'm so embarrassed," he said. "I've been struggling, you know, with my design for a Citizen of the World Passport. I believe you'd find it of interest. But it's much too amateurish to show you at this point. I haven't got the pattern worked out. Doves flying over a rainbow is what I'm aiming for."

"Nice," I said, lighting up. "I'd like to see it sometime. What's this room we're in?"

"The command-and-control bunker. The missiles are next door." I invited him to smoke, but he declined. "Want to know a secret?"

Who didn't?

"That horsewhip my wife carries. The one everybody thinks was Emma Goldman's. She bought it in 1962 at Abercrombie and Fitch. She brags about it behind your backs. Don't let her get your goat. She's just an old humbug."

On the strength of this intimate confession, however embittered or even fraudulent, I presumed to ask him to carry up to his wife, at his leisure, a message as to where I awaited her; for, upon leaving her after dinner, I had taken as a promise her droll "See you later, alligator."

8.

Poor Guy had at once diplomatically complied, and not five minutes later Grace Brissenden confronted me in the bunker.

Her half-smile of willingness to seek *détente* was perhaps an illusion projected by my wishful thinking, to judge from the way she impatiently flicked her thigh with the now questionably anarchist horsewhip.

Cleverly I began by conceding a moot point. "I only want to congratulate you," I said, "on being right. It *is* May; she *has* changed; she's grown hopelessly dull and insufferable; she must therefore be Gilbert Long's mistress."

"What are you saying?"

"You remember our talks—about the redistribution of mental wealth."

"I'm sure I don't know what you mean when you use such jargon."

She *was* sharp; the "jargon" accusation was my Achilles heel. I would have to be more emotionally open. "Darling Grace," I said, "we're alone, you and I. You needn't pretend with me. We're old friends."

"Don't be mushy." She was ice cold.

"The masquerade," I said more harshly, "is over."

"Masquerade?"

"That travesty at dinner."

"That was no masquerade," she said. "We simply are as we appear. Sometimes, you know," she continued, "you won't see things that aren't—"

"Aren't there?"

"No, that aren't as you wish they were. It makes people uncomfortable. They feel you expect them to be—"

"Better than they seem?"

"Better than they *are!* They feel you reproach them. And then they feel tired of feeling reproached, and then they feel like standing up for what they are."

"And as for what they *were?*"

"Oh, I don't deny it. We've all changed—all but you. We've seen the *light*."

Was her emphasis a challenge to fight also over who owned which metaphors? I countered with one of theirs. "I don't choose to 'stand up' merely to salute the flag of my inalienable right to be no better than I am." Yet in her imputation to me of guilt, I felt something of my old tendency to wallow; *had* I irritated them to reaction? Grace had me on the run. But at that instant she inexplicably retreated, to make a grab for territory I had abandoned as strategically worthless:

"You're the one who's wrong," she said, "about May Server. It's not May; it's not anybody; there's no such thing. It was all just a game, an academic exercise in logistics, and now you won't pack up your tent but insist on crouching there with your inaccurate hand-drawn guerrilla maps of nothing, crowing over the success of some hypothetical ambush."

"Is that how you see me? As so ineffectually beside the point?"

She pondered. "No, I believe you're more dangerous than that. I think . . . I think you're a Commie!"

It was then that I saw how to make her play it out. "Where," I asked, "do you get your intelligence?"

"You know I can't reveal that."

"Have you sunk so low," I charged, "that you resort to claiming your so-called evidence comes from unidentified persons?"

"Ah, you know me too well. Civil liberties to the rescue. Very well, you shall have it: *I'm* my source. I know I'm right, because—because I know how I'm terribly *wrong*."

"How is that?"

"Domestically."

"I don't follow," I said. "Isn't it—our disagreement—basically on matters of foreign policy?"

"I'm not talking about that now, you idiot. I mean domestically in my domestic life. That's where I'm wrong. Look, you've gone sniffing around after people's private affairs—well, then, if you want so much to know, snap to attention. Gilbert Long and I—do I have to spell it out?"

"And poor—"

"Poor Guy? Yes, I drove him over the brink, or rather so far away from the brink that it amounts to the same thing. He persuaded himself that my marital infidelity is an inevitable by-product of my dread of nuclear extinction."

"How miserable he must be!"

"You tender-headed fool—he's deliriously happy, he and his little May. I make them possible. It's I—it's *we*—who give them cause to huddle, quivering together like baby rabbits. They're ideally matched. They're a couple of children! Why, they're upstairs in her room right now, making crayon drawings and pasting each other's pictures in old passports. And we protect them, you see, from people like *you* who might upset them. And so we are, in ways you don't appreciate, immensely loyal."

"And your loyalty to the truth? To the ideal we once shared that every person has the capacity for—has the *right* to—the clear, bright consciousness that . . . that"—I was groping for eloquence, and a phrase came into my head—"that the person who steals your pants still gets into them one leg at a time?"

"Tell it to your Commie friends!" she said. "Good night!"

She turned, but I brought her around with my next shot: "If you don't believe, isn't it hypocritical to keep *that?*" And I indicated the horsewhip, though now convinced of its strictly commercial provenance.

"I suppose *you* want it, to chastise some poor leftie heretic who strays from the party line of the week. Have you forgotten that even your precious Emma, radical to the end, renounced the Bolshies?"

"No, but have *you* forgotten that she didn't shop at Abercrombie and Fitch?"

She didn't turn a whisker. "My plan is to donate it to a museum." Without warning, she tossed it to me. "It's yours, darling. *You're* a museum." And she was gone for good.

It was freezing in the bunker, but I hardly felt it, so acutely conscious was I of, above my head, the former site of the gazebo where Grace and I had together boogalooed. She still knew how to keep me on my toes. I had twice her *élan,* though, and was infinitely more promising. What I hadn't mastered was her timing.

The Revised Dictionary of Slang and Uncontrollable English

PREFACE

This new edition is the result of a contractual obligation and of my proximity to the English language for the many years during which I was preparing this edition. It is designed to form a monumental companion to that humble work *The Little Book of Pocket Words* (Gulf & Western University Press), at present the regrettable authority for standard English. From the Oxford English Dictionary (Oxford Home Box Office, now out of print, sadly) and Webster's New International Dictionary, Second Edition (alas, almost universally shredded or consumed as roll-your-own fireplace logs), as well as from diligent correspondents throughout the British Commonwealth and the U.S., I am proud to have learnt numerous terms, among them (reluctantly omitted here due to funding limitations) some forty or fifty thousand additional words and phrases which, on prolonged scrutiny, may be thought to connote some form of coital adjacency.

Here I am keen to give the proportions of entries:

Unpleasantries	50%
Repulsivisms	35%
Toilet articles	6%
Bad words	6%
Septics	2%
Unsavories	1%

Should the more distressing entries have been rendered in euphemism? This is the practice once followed by scholarly practitioners. My rule has been to deal with them only as salaciously as is required under the terms of my contractual obligation; in a few instances, I have had to suppress my natural tastefulness by means of flogging.

Finally, it is a pleasure to thank, for items that might well have been overlooked, Mr. Julyan Franklin, author of *A Lexicography of All the Pornographic Words in This Title;* Rev. Franklyn Julian, author of *A Water-Closet Medley;* Mrs. Jewel Lynn Frank, who generously shared notes for her work in progress, *The Rough Stuff;* and "Julia" of New Zealand— zealous rememberer, leechlike gatherer.

about time, or **a.t.** Approximate time of day; freq. employed by unemployed or by persons so sympathetic to unemployment that they use the argot as a matter of principle. *Times,* "'I will have a further announcement at 4 a.t.,' said Mrs. Thatcher."—2. In gen. idiom. use when speaker is neurologically incapable of knowing or discovering the time, as in (e.g., during tantrum, coital climax, etc.) *It's about time!*—3. Hence, any agreement to meet for coitus at an unspecified future time. Princess G. Kelly, *National Enquirer,* "I always had an a.t. with Elvis."

academic robes, all dressed up in, with no papers to grade, or

with no texts to deconstruct, etc. Unemployed.—2. Sexually aroused but unable to secure any coital associate, due to unemployment.

bore me with the details, don't! Omit the preliminaries to coitus!: low U.S. Senate use.

butt fell off, he would go crazy if his. Said of an unreliable or excitable person: U.S. high literary.

dick-on-the-mutton. Any male affianced or annexed for the purpose of ready availability of coital junction. Prob. New Zealand.

fine print. A diminutive harlot.—2. The female incunabula.

get a job. To offer oneself or a member of one's family for professional coitus. Undergraduate patois, ca. Long Vacation of 1960–84.

Giant's Causeway. Marginally interesting potential subject for coital toleration. Ex S. Johnson (in Boswell), on the G. C., "Worth seeing? Yes; but not worth going to see."

good copulation enough, this was a. Colloq., incorrect for "This was a good dinner enough, to be sure; but it was not a dinner to *ask* a man to." S. Johnson (in Boswell).

haddock-and-Velveeta. Underwater coitus; Cockney rhyming s., ex apothecaries' Latin *aqua velva,* after-shave lotion made of water from the bath of a prostitute.

legal defense fund. Any law firm whose members practice advocacy coitus.

Millie Rem. A wanton female who invites or solicits coitus with nuclear technicians, core attendants, site inspectors, etc.—2. Hence, U.S., any Nuclear Regulatory Commission member.

Mr. Used before a surname to emphasize that the male thus designated devotes much time to coitus. Obs. except—2. In business use, often as *"Hello, Mr._____!",* to impute moral laxity.

nice but not national health insurance. Very abominably distasteful: usu. said after enjoyment of conjugal congress or observation of the female ursa major.

on hold. In state of having recently enacted *coitus obstructus.*—2. Hence, in any condition of expectation, vertigo, lycanthropy, or malpractice.—3. Presumed dead or extinct. R. T. Peterson, *A Field Guide to Drawings of Birds,* "The species is on hold."

oxbow incident. Undue coitus, usu. that which damages, weakens, or excites the partners very considerably. Ex 1810 U.S. social disorder incited by the 74th Foot Regiment of the Montana Light Infantry.

park. Fuck. Ex (by analogy), as H. Hefner (after Marcus Aurelius) insists, Greek ρφκε, lit. to poke rhythmically until parallel with the curb. Cf. *parker, park off, to park over, park you!, park you, Jack!, go park yourself!,* and *what the park.*

please sit down! Please cease attempting vertical coitus aboard the aircraft!

stamp collector. A woman attending Postal Service dances year after year.—2. A postal official's trull.

surgeon general's office. Any place where a tobacco addict or addicts can smoke the drug; a pad.—2. The female penumbra: some New Zealand hobo use.

take a meeting. Fly to California for the purpose of engaging in coitus.

take care now. Park off!

two Ping-pong balls and a fish. Any Chinese motion picture.—2. A popular meal consisting of two croquettes made of minced seafood molded around a plastic or styrofoam globular base to add lightness and size; R. Carver, *Take My Order . . . Please!,* "Gimme a coupla Ping-pongs-and-fish." By 1984, any round or oval item of fast food, esp. when consumed before, during, or after coitus.—3. In baseball, a pitching strategy whereby each of the first two pitches bounces once, and the third is thrown in such a manner that it gravitates toward the nearest body of water. *N.Y. Times,* "Neil Allen Too Controlled," "Unless the once volatile young man gets back in touch with his emotions, regaining his fast Ping-pong, curve Ping-pong, and slider fish, he threatens to become a chilly 25–0 statistic and lose his acceptance by the fans."—4. Hence, any acceptable male delicti.

undersecretary. The male rotunda. Gen. in pl.; N. Mailer, *Ancient Briefings,* "Had not his small staff two fine hirsute undersecretaries to its credit?"

well qualified. Very eccentric; insane. Usu. implies that the person so characterized participates in excessive coitus. Cf. the (mainly Australian) proverbial saying "His cock needs no etymologist."

Coming Apart
at the Semes

For half a century, NEWSWEEK has reported on the news and the people who made it. . . . But in this anniversary issue, the focus is different: on the men and women who have not made these great events, but lived them. . . . This extraordinary saga of five heartland families . . . whose lives testify to what our country has been and is becoming . . . is richer and more compelling than fiction. . . . Dreams die hard among a people who . . . have never known when to surrender.
—*Newsweek* Special Anniversary Issue, Spring 1983

For half a decade, AXES has been a quarterly forum for discourse on artistic praxis and those who praxe it. But at this time, we wish to appropriate a strategy long co-opted by that tacky bourgeois journalism which, prerogativing the dominant philistinisms, is swamped at this juncture by its own compromised tissues. This anniversary supplement is an (extra)plastic conflatulation of the contextic community as a triad of paradigmal kinship units: the Baxters, a staunch clan of obsolete modernists; the Russos, an irrepressible tribe of decadent expressionists; and the Joneses, an oppressed but indomitable household of duped retrograde humanists. These women and nonwomen, who have not made texts but lived them, are a hyperbolized exemplarization of what our critical discourse is resolutely becoming.

THE TOWN THAT AFFIRMED ITSELF

It was 1929, a temporal reference point, and John Baxter, in his sixty-sixth year, sat gazing out an interstice of the cultural framework he had built with his own hands in a space called the United States of America. Born Jean Baxtre, the son of a humble sweeper at the Salon des Refusés in Paris, he had emigrated in 1880 and founded Paree, Ohio—in those days little more than a pictorial field, miles from the nearest mainstream. The Absence in his empty pockets signified the Presence of a dream: a dream of boundlessness, of fruited planes from which the work might forge beyond illusionism, perhaps, eventually crossing the frontier of the edge. By 1913, he had won a defense contract for the Armory Show, and throughout the 1920s his shop ground out a profitable line. A man of rigorous taste, who would have been disgusted by his employees' display of vulgar mimesis behind his back, he won respect for what came to be called the Baxter Style—an extension of his own formalist demeanor and white-on-white haberdashery. "Each of us got a pencil," a former Baxter & Co. draftsman recalled in notes for a *festschrift,* "and when it wore out, Old Man B.— what a funny guy! He told us to take a supreme leap into theory!"

Now, on the date that was called October 24, 1929, a tide of red ink was defacing the purism of John Baxter's dream. As he sat reflexing, he discoursed to himself that his wife and teenage son would inherit merely a problemous residue. He was dying, and with him a post-innocence was passing, too. He heard a Voice foretelling not only his own closure but that of his heirs: *The family plot.* Perhaps none of them would ever escape the worst tyranny of all—the tyranny of narrative.

THE GREAT REPRESSION

By 1933, the vortex of change was in full flush. But Mario Russo knew only a surge of gratuitous individual pathos at the way his wife, Maria, and their two kids, Tony and Theresa, were suffocating in the headwinds of Social Realism. Twelve years earlier, on a crowded ship, he had caught his first glimpse of the Ellis Island *doxa*. An illiterate exile in flight from a harsh culture confined to the fossilized Masterpiece mode of Dante, he cradled in his hairy, muscular arms a frail ideal: the total liberation of gesture. Old Baxter had patronized him as an honorably vital polarity. But Baxter was dead, and one by one the Baxter ideas were going into receivership. With Old Mrs. Baxter drifting into an irrelevant neoclassical coda, Junior Baxter took charge, struck a deal with a remote relative in France named Tristan Tzara, and retooled to manufacture syntactic bullets. Excitedly, Mario agreed to subcontract the requisite velvet jackets. But at the bank, he learned that Tzara had paid in non-negotiable coin called revolt.

Nobody's schema was going according to plan. The ghetto residents, Wilma and Arthur Jones, had migrated North with the dream of internalizing the values of their oppressors. Now, pedagogues trying to transplant into Paree's children the artificial heart of humanism, they feared they were losing their own boy, Pip. One winter day in 1937, the toddler had stood for hours in the terminus, watching for a train on which a mythic figure called Lionel Trilling was modulating horizontally to Chicago. When it passed by, Pip waved, but Trilling didn't validate him. It was as if all the old *données* were suddenly demystified. Pip turned wild, running with a gang of disingenuously self-styled radicals—precocious serialists from posh Tone Row. There was no discoursing what the future held, as the reactionary narrative tightened its hold upon each and every one.

THE FIGHT FOR THE CONFLICTUAL TERRAIN

On December 9, 1941, Maria Russo, a fading archetype of what was then called Beauty, was fetishizing her hair. She wanted to look nice for her daughter Theresa's wedding, unaware that inscribed in the photographs of this banal ceremony of spurious transcendence, future generations would see a tipsy mother of the bride making of herself both spectacle and anti-spectacle. Then came a Voice: *Mama!* She turned to find her eighteen-year-old Tony in the uniform of the Derrière Garde. For the next four years, she was unable to distanciate herself from that which she still called Emotion.

The axis was in full tilt. With his fellow conscripts, Tony viewed a filmic medical warning about propadeutic precautions and, of course, about cinema itself. Then, misled by elite elements, he took part in the imperialistic campaign against Japanese superinscription of the surface. Junior Baxter, too, smelled the stench of bootlessness, in wave after wave of para-literary airborne assaults behind party lines, while Arthur Jones was held captive in the P.O.W.-camp stage set of a Broadway play's capitalistic verisimilitude. None of them had foreseen that the real struggle was in their own backyards—in the torrid, stifling tropes of the fascist narrative.

REFORMATTING THE FUTURE

It was a time of categories of figuration masquerading as Truth—a time when the media hypnotocracy dominatized the masses with the famous inconclusive exchange of views between Cleanth Brooks and F. W. Bateson on Wordsworth's "A slumber did my spirit seal," implicating towns like Paree in the nationwide scandal of Reason. Yet, unwittingly, even Paree's parochial robots were propagating a new agenda, the Code War, whose enterprise was no less than a thriving network of signs, with flashing signifiers at every intersection. Before long, Main Street consumers would stroll heedlessly through their own Grande Syntagmatique.

Mario Russo hired on as a driver for Junior Baxter's new fleet of metataxis. Plenty of fares obtained, and most of them looked the other way when Mario opportunistically made change in a counterfeit currency called Style. But such "liberals" were in for a shock. On January 1, 1953, Theresa Russo's husband Axel fell into a fissure between two trace structures and disappeared. In the confusion that followed, Theresa inadvertently married her own brother, Tony, and incestuously proliferated the Russo line into the next generation: an exploitative pseudo-event manufactured by the narrative's pornographic Allure to deflect attention from its bogus Depth, which had claimed Axel as its first victim.

AN ERA OF IRRUPTION

Be-bop-a-lula was what it sounded like to the adults—the gnomic utterance of a luxury commodity called Herman's Hermeneutics. Soon Pip Jones and other dropouts from the Academy were alienating their elders by rapping in the weird new lingua and hanging out at the juncture. On July 4, 1964, in a back seat with a boy from the wrong side of the grid, Theresa Russo fought vainly against her first taste of textuality.

The same night, Pip's mother, Wilma, succumbed to the ideology of the Devil in human form—a used-paperback hero by the name of William Empson. Wilma, a seemingly static matrix, secretly enjoyed sitting in the dark and letting ambiguities take wing, and she was ripe for seduction by Empson— not just by the platinum incandescence of his erotics but by his sheer star quality and perhaps, too, by the fragile shadow of William Shakespeare just below the skin of the exegesis. *Wil-*

ma/William, chanted a Voice inside her as she strove narcissis-
tically to invoke a reciprocal similitude with the internal structures of Greatness. That night she meaningfully packed her
bags and vanished into the substrate of interpretation, an already moribund hegemony from whose zone she could be re-
trieved by precisely no one. And the narrative, in its totalitarian pretense that something else will happen, marched on.

THE BLIND RAGE FOR UNITY

In the full cry of the erosion to come, trying to understand
what had gone wrong, people would say it was with the extinction of the figure-ground relationship that the fear began. By
1969, even the marginally prescient Junior Baxter was anxious,
passing up the chance to invest in a go-go European-import
corporation that soon made fortunes by marketing the rights to
the word "valorize." By the time his symptoms were diagnosed
as high-modernist irony, he was sterile. His marriage, with an
aging ex-model named Rose Sélavy, would be troubled for
years, until they adopted a conceptual baby. Mario Russo, in
his more manneristic audacity, began privileging whiskey and
women, and driving at reckless speeds along vertiginous era-
sures. He was worried about Tony and Theresa, whom the
paternalistic narrative had written off until they decided what
to do with their lives. Maria voyeuristically looked after her
grandchildren: Debbie was caught up in the craze for the function of desire, and its production, while Rocco hovered peril-
ously on the fringes of violent demonstrations against the
zoom lens and deep focus at the nearby methodological base.

Then, on March 15, 1970, Tony reappeared in order to en-
gage in a necessary act of parricide. In France, of course, that
choice would have more than justified bravos, but in banal
Paree the townspeople sentimentally inflected the death of the

old, tokenizing their own passive submission to the senile authoritarianism of the narrative.

ENDURING A NEW PROBLEMATIC

The avalanches of uncertainty whirled closer, beginning to ebb away at the town's monuments to its own futility. It was as if these Midwesterners were being asked to pay, in the inflated dollars of self-deception, for the errors of the petit-mandarin class and its Westernized presuppositions back East. In 1972, hit with an intolerable increase in parataxes, the local earthworks closed down. Pip Jones lingered at the edge of the crowd that gathered for a last look at the great brown facticity. Then the reductivists stomped in to obliterate it with a flood of bankrupt dialectic. Pip decided to de-originate himself: *Hey, maybe if I go far enough I can embody my own critique!* He ran away to enroll in the New York School, earning the tuition by working with time in various ways. This child of a discredited tradition felt almost at home in his new neighborhood, the minimalist Dead End, where from his window he could see the Transavangardia and the Spiral of Infinite Regress, clogged with new vehicles for the previously unspeakable, and everywhere the concerned faces of the revolutionaries who had finally dared to pronounce the weekly belletrism of Jack Kroll irremediably defunct. One day, agog in Central Park, his feet crunching the shells of nourishing zoösemiotic peanuts, Pip thought he saw the fugitive Tony Russo melt away into a crowd of image scavengers. "Hi!" he yelled, whereupon the authorities slapped him into the prison house of language. Not till 1982 was he sent home on provisional release (*parole*).

Why didn't you stop it! echoed a Voice within him as he tumbled from the remorseless freight train of the phallocratic narrative into the waiting arms of his father. But the once proud humanism of Arthur Jones had been exposed as a hollow imposturocratization. At the local movie house the week before, he had helplessly watched his former pupil Theresa Russo up there on the screen in a momentary blaze of celluloid fantasy before she was flattened by a foregrounding device. The next day, he had seen those still good-looking collections of nerve stimuli Rose Baxter and Maria Russo run out of town by a mob of post-Puritans, and a headline in the post-*Post* about Maria's two grandchildren fatally annulled by an unapprehended Other. He had seen the town's leading citizen, Junior Baxter, in a suicidal bid to renounce (and thus, of course, to authenticize) his father's modernist dream, hurl himself repeatedly against a picture plane till it gave way and sent him plunging to his doom, impaled on a fraudulent vanishing point. Now, sensing that the hierarchical narrative was driving to its climax, Arthur clutched his stomach in one of his recurrent attacks of diegesis, and terminated.

At home, Pip faced what he naively continued to call Facts. Paree was a ghost town, the Jones homestead a decomposing shack. *My only hope is to go into interior decorization. A few armchair ideas, parlor pink, important mirrors ... And video —lots and lots of video.* He positioned himself in a hot bath and played briefly with an interrogation of the aesthetic possibilities of inserting a video feedback coil into the medium of water. *Pip ... piP ...* And that was all.

Or was it? We have forgotten about Junior Baxter's conceptual baby—but the narrative, in its hornswoggling Complexity, has not. Literalized into a five-year-old girl called Mary Baxter, a reification of the unquenchable spirit of delusion, she crept surreptitiously toward the Jones house and its tepid bathwater, all the while rending the Silence with her prattle of naughty words: *Once upon a time ...*

Supreme Court Roundup

Record Review

The Supreme Court refused to hear an appeal by
former President Richard M. Nixon from a ruling by
the United States Court of Appeals under which
large portions of some 6,000 hours of White House
tape recordings will eventually be released
to the public.
—*The New York Times*, November 30, 1982

PICK HIT: The Benefit Concert   MUST TO AVOID: Bad Rap

**Nixon, Haldeman & Dean: *Blunder Down the Road* (District of
Columbia)** Not up to their *Smoking Gun* debut, though audio-
wiz producer Alex Butterfield's notorious "walls of sound" remain serviceable. The B side is dismissable on the merits, but
with Dick's country-bluesy growl on "Can of Worms" and
Brushcut Bob's proto-new-wave incantation of "$900,000,"
Side One will pass as professional heat-taking at its baddest. If
bad is as good as they get on this outing, that's as it should be,
and the profundo-paranoiac high of Nixon/Dean's smoochfest-
as-dialectic "They Are Asking for It/What an Exciting Pros-

pect" didn't change my mind. Bet they didn't change theirs either. **B MINUS**

Nixon & Dean: *Bad Rap* **(Panmunjom import)** The biggest ripoff of this or any century, with no less than nine of ten cuts mere soup's-on rephrasings of Nixon's own '50s and '60s anthems (all six extended-play "Crises" plus "Anna Chennault," "Hoover Told Me," and the man's all-purpose signature tune, the self-fulfilling "This Thing Burns My Tail"). When Tricky isn't covering himself, he's covering Janis Joplin's "Bobby Was a Ruthless (Characterization Bleeped)," a charisma-grab not half as perverse as smoothie Dean's foray into faux-gospel backup antiphonies ("Absolutely!" "Totally true!" "That's correct!"), musically O.K.—Tormé meets Torquemada—but commercially misguided. **D MINUS**

Nixon, Dean & Haldeman: *The Benefit Concert* **(Creep)** You can't play jailhouse mariachi with church-charity-bazaar chops, but these guys can—and did, in the definitive March 21, 1973, concert to aid prisoners of conscience victimized by Sirica-style justice. Unified by the rhythmically haunting Latin-fluence of former house band Liddy & His Cubans while aspiring to the bigger, cleaner sound of Vesco & the Mexican Laundry, the gang finds its groove in a three-route statement melding socio-folkie concern ("How Much Money Do You Need?"), absurdist riffs ("Who Is Porter?"), and spiritual smarts ("As God Is My Maker/We Need More Money")—for sheer ride-this-thing-out staying power, the greatest album of all time. Dean, in superb voice (shoo-in airplay hit: "Cancer"), comes into his own as a soloist forever peerless even by the standard later set in the legendary Capitol Hill sessions. El Tricko, feeling his Quaker oats, pours on that baritone cream and serves up instant classic ("It Is Wrong That's for Sure"), while Haldeman brings home the metaphysical bacon with late-breaking robotica-sardonica, *viz.* "fatal flaw/verbal evil/ stupid human errors/dopes," and none dare call it doowop. Not that all this means I have to like it, but I love it. And they almost get away with it. **A**

Nixon, Dean, Haldeman & Ehrlichman: *Wild Scenario* **(Enemies List Productions)** Search-and-seize tempos, thesaurus lyrics about "furtherance" and "concomitance"—as long as they kept breaking a few simple rules, there was no reason why this ensemble couldn't parlay its deeply involved harmonies into a pure celebration of criminal liability or even better. Ehrlichman's showboat presence here is an acoustic plus, and though his surprisingly apt cover of Liza's "That Problem Goes On and On" hardly bespeaks the "deep six" poet whose witty improvs would quasi-compensate for the group's ultimately fatal loss of the Dean pipes, it wears far better than Nixon's descent into bubblegum-maudlin, "We Can't Harm These Young People"—so indictably undanceable that you ignore it at your own peril. **B**

Big Enchilada (N.Y. Bar Association) How you respond to this morose tribute compilation depends on your tolerance for cross-referential portentousness (Kleindienst's "Mitchell and I," Haldeman's "Cover Up for John") and ye-olde-memory-lane perfunctoriana (the Chief's "Good Man"): the sky's the limit on my own tolerance for sodden wee-hours-in-the-studio sentimentality about an aging master-performer never adequately recorded in his own right. I'd feel better, though, about Henry Petersen wailing "LaRue broke down and cried like a baby/Not fully he broke down/But when it came to testifying about John Mitchell/He just broke down and started to cry" if Petersen knew as much about blues changes as he does about

LaRue's tear ducts, or if I knew as much about Mitchell as I would if somebody had bothered to mike him where the moon don't shine. Still, on this one they make you care, or at least they would if they knew how. **B MINUS**

Nixon, Haldeman, Ehrlichman, Dean & Mitchell: *Inaudible* **(Sony)** Dumb title, and every word of it is true. Either Butterfield was asleep at the switch or this is a concept move for the Japanese abstraction market—a waste of vinyl and, with Mitchell sitting in, an even worse waste of Enchilada exotica. Giveaway: "Yeah, yeah—the way, yeah, yeah, I understand. Postponed—right, right, yeah/Yeah, yeah/Right/Yeah/(Inaudible)." But they've never sounded looser. **C PLUS**

Nixon & Kleindienst: *Let's Stand Up for People* **(Grand Jury)** This tortured after-you-Alphonse act recycles the basics of limited-hang-out obscurity into strategically meaningless polyrhythms aching to transcend their own pungency. That a lot of it is artfully incoherent must mean Dick & Dick thought the long-overdue synthesis might just come naturally, but the album divides too neatly into standard-issue I-know-you-know hooks, standard-issue you-know-I-know hooks, and standard-issue I-thought-you-ought-to-know-I-know-you-know hooks, plus a defiantly throwaway A-side opener, "Would You Like Coffee? Coca-Cola?"—one of those ersatz-icky coat-the-palate numbers played with such jumpy, nerve-jangled insincerity that it leaves you nursing few illusions about this pair's ability to cross over to simple pop truths. **C MINUS**

Nixon & Dean: *The Dean Farewell Tour* **(Washington Post)** You want soulful resignation, they've got soulful resignation, and they've got it with spark (fave: "Feet to the Fire"). You want the rush of live jamming, they've got that too, with sound effects ("I Am Sorry, Steve, I Hit the Wrong Bell"). Fun's fun, but this is a major partnership's final stamp on an electronic heritage. **A MINUS**

Nixon, Rogers, Haldeman & Ehrlichman: *Really Ticklish* **(Dash)** Even more painful than was intended. People may sleep easier thinking sideman Rogers was the turnoff element here, but the group was already so beset by personnel instability that distinctions are moot. Synth-zomboid Haldeman's "Facade of Normal Operations" represses more than I wish it knew, and only Ehrlichman brightens the funk, mustering a virtually Segrettiesque playfulness for two Randy Newman–type persona pieces, "Suspend These Birds" and "Dean Is Some Little Clerk." Maybe I'm taking it personally, but it seems to the Dean of American Rock Critics, a.k.a. Some Other Little Clerk, that the dream was over, and not a point in time too soon. **F PLUS**

Indecent Indemnity

Author's Note: Everything in this account has been meticulously found out from people.

Nettie,* a blowsy blonde of thirty-seven, slowed her blue Oldsmobile Custom Cruiser for Exit 23 of the Del Morta Freeway, feeling the late-day Southern California sun move off her face as she made the turn. It was 7:18 P.M., Thursday, August 4, 1977, when she passed the working-class community of El Clangas and, just outside town, pulled up to the trailer where Barton Keyes perversely chose to live.

Keyes, vice-president in charge of claims investigation for General Fidelity of California, a division of Norton Promotions, Inc., a wholly owned subsidiary of Norton, Ltd., was a skinflint. He would not even let the company hire a secretary for him—if he needed a little typing, he buzzed Nettie over from sales—and he had a maverick's disdain of his peers' taste for Tudor mansions stuffed with Gainsboroughs. He had always found insurance society too flashy for his blood. He preferred a quiet evening with a statistical printout, a perpetual calendar, and a volume of Freud, scorning the tinseled carousing at the fancy underwriter hangouts in the Hills.

As Nettie exerted a downward pressure on her Oldsmobile's inside door handle, Keyes came out to greet her—a short,

---

*Where a participant has no surname or given name, none has been fabricated.

stocky man of fifty, often mistaken for Edward G. Robinson. Nettie had phoned ahead to say that while working late, transcribing his dictation from a Dictola microcassette, she had come across something that confused and bothered her. Now she handed him the cassette—a gray, rectangle-shaped capsule, no bigger than a child's bar of soap, with the data concealed inside circular flanges on a continuous magnetic-oxide loop.

"Come on in and get a load off your feet," said Keyes. "How about a cup of joe?" He made instant coffee, then fitted the cassette into the extra machine he kept at home in case anybody should ever come over with anything bothersome on a tape. In silence, the two listened to Keyes' dictation. Minute particulars of his monthly expenses for July. (Nettie could hear his irritation at having to clear the $32.50 with the company president, young Norton.) A note to the district attorney, thanking him for cooperation in a court hearing—routine, rote phrases of courtesy which Nettie found tiresome to listen to when she was waiting for the part of the tape that bothered her. A draft of comments on a legal brief in which the company alleged fraud on the part of an electric-power-company lineman named Roy Neary, whom Keyes had long suspected of lying about having his truck totaled in a close encounter with UFOs.

"This is the one," said Nettie suddenly. It was a different man's voice—a confession of homicide, addressed to Keyes, describing in lurid detail the speaker's plot with one Phyllis Dietrichson to insure her husband against accident, murder him, make it look as if he had fallen from a railroad train, and collect double indemnity. Keyes knew of the Dietrichson claim. It reeked to the skies. But he had been obsessed with the bizarre Neary case.

Now his eyebrows lifted in surmise. "That voice—it's Walter, isn't it?"

"Maybe it sounds like him and maybe it doesn't," said Nettie. Walter Neff, a go-getting insurance salesman of thirty-five, was her regular boss—and Keyes' protégé.

Keyes switched off the machine. "That's funny," he said. "Well, don't worry about it. It must be nothing."

Myth: The insurance racket today is more modern than that of yesteryear. *Fact:* In spite of computers that grow ever more prolific in spewing out facts, the traditional scams and swindles motivated by passions of sex, bloodlust, jealousy, and a morbid fascination with Death have never died.

Myth: By 1970, slimy insurance practices were largely regulated by federal and local governments. *Fact:* The fundamental process of getting someone to sign a contract for insurance without knowing what he is signing is more arcane and complex than ever. The use of computers and video simulations, especially to teach methods of ingeniously slipping such contracts into innocent-looking stacks of papers awaiting signature, reached a peak in 1977, when social critic Christopher Lasch wrote, "Not one person in ten has the slightest understanding that one out of three times he signs his name, he has bought accident insurance."

On Friday, August 5, Keyes played the murder confession for the head of the General Fidelity legal department, Shapiro.

"This doesn't really jog my memory," said Shapiro.

"Doesn't it sound like Walter Neff?" said Keyes.

"Are you kidding?" said Shapiro. "It must be Nettie imitating Walter's voice—some kind of gag. Let me put it in my safe, where I have some other laughs I'm saving for Keswick [the corporation counsel] when he comes out to the Coast."

"Don't bother," said Keyes. "It's probably just a guy with Walter's same vocal timbre."

Deeply fond of Walter, Keyes had one tragic flaw: his insights into human psychology tended not to encompass the assumption that his brilliant protégé would suddenly commit murder.

The next morning, a Saturday, Keyes reluctantly went into the deserted office to pull Walter Neff's files for scrutiny. The watchman, Joe Pete, let him into Walter's cubicle.

"Some kind of misdemeanor going on, Mr. Keyes?" asked Joe Pete.

"It's O.K., Joe Pete," said Keyes. "It's possible he's confessed to murder, but we're handling it."

"Holy mackerel!" said Joe Pete.

Walter Neff's files were suggestive but clean as a whistle. The office grapevine would later dub them "the Harlequin Romances."

Four days later, on August 9, Nettie found another confession on the machine. At the end, the voice said, "It takes a hell of a long time to unburden myself of all this, Keyes. Why don't you just have me arrested and end this living hell that I, Walter Neff, am living in?"

That afternoon at 3:30, young Norton, the president of General Fidelity, flew back from the parent company's headquarters in New York to meet with Keyes and Shapiro, the legal-department head, to discuss the progress of the Neary case. Keyes was in seventh heaven about it. Roy Neary had signed an affidavit about being attacked at night on a lonely road by a fleet of UFOs whose mischievous swooping and darting and red-hot glow caused $7,879 worth of mechanical and electrical damage to his yellow power-company pickup truck—the kind of seemingly neat, airtight story that Keyes' study of psychosis had trained him to distrust. He was just itching to get Neary onto a witness stand and confront him with astrophysical charts from NASA. The Walter situation, though, was a pin-prick in his enjoyment.

On the way into the meeting, he took young Norton aside and said, "I suppose Shapiro told you about the tape that sounds like Walter Neff confessing to the murder of Dietrich-son?"

Young Norton looked icily at his longtime inferior. He made a mental note to cover himself by sending a predated memo advising Keyes to investigate Neff. Then he said, "I almost recollect something about something along those lines. This is no time for office pranks, Keyes. Whatever it is, take care of it."

Keyes nodded, and thought, *Big shot. I'll get you for this.*

Barton Keyes had spent his whole life working for the Norton family, helping his father, old man Keyes, sweep up for old Mr. Norton, whose grocery in the old neighborhood in Boston's South End mushroomed into a chain of supermarkets bought out in 1939 by Wall Street executive-talent scavenger Lou ("The Cannibal") Lorraine, who put old Mr. Norton at the head of LouLor Industries' insurance division out in L.A. while young Keyes, toiling as a clerk in Cambridge, shined young Harvard student Norton's shoes in exchange for access to his abnormal-psychology textbooks and slide rule—a cama-raderie further modified by public insinuations of young Nor-ton's father's links to organized-crime figures, notably parole violator Legs Diamond and creative financier Vladimir Arcati, whose casino activities in various Belgian Congo banks en-abled him to be the very same man who lent old Norton bags and bags of money to buy out the insurance company, reincor-porate in New York as a public utility, put himself, his son young Norton, the same Arcati, and a Boston lawyer named Keswick on the board of directors, and send the street-smart young Barton Keyes out to the Coast to do insurance-claims investigation, paying him in preferred stock. They were all well aware by then that old man Keyes had been overlooked, but young Keyes was the only one who never forgot it.

Keyes had been avoiding Walter's office, but the next morning, August 10, he went in there with his container of "joe" and the new cassette. Walter looked terrible. The Fred MacMurray-ish verve was subdued, his hair was unkempt, his skin clammy, and blood trickled down his temple. Keyes had seen enough fishy injury cases to recognize a laceration inflicted by a woman's ankle bracelet.

"Walter," said Keyes, "I hate to bust in with such a ridiculous, nitpicking question, but did you accidentally use Nettie's machine to confess to the murder of Dietrichson?"

"If you say so. But I honestly don't recall making the tapes."

"Repression," said Keyes. "Classic. O.K., do you remember bumping off Dietrichson at all?"

"Vaguely. Well, no. I guess not."

"Why confess on tape, then? That's cuckoo, Walter."

"I'm sorry—it sounds irrational, but I just can't accept that I did something as nuts as murder."

"I know. Maybe you confessed just to act out a general, underlying sense of guilt. So—am I going to find any more of these tapes?"

"No, no—I swear on my mother's policy, Keyes, there won't be any more."

"I hope not," said Keyes. "And have the company doc take a gander at that head wound."

On a hunch, Keyes went back to the office that night. At 1 A.M. he passed a dozing Joe Pete and took the elevator. Keyes' light was on. Through the door he saw Walter leaning over the Dictola and bleeding profusely through his shirt. Apparently someone has shot him, Keyes mused.

Keyes made a phone call. Then he said to Walter, "They're on their way."

Walter said, "You know why you couldn't figure this one, Keyes? I'll tell you. Because the guy you were looking for was too close. He was right across the desk from you."

"Closer than that, Walter."

"I love you, too," said Walter. "O.K., out of personal loyalty to you, I'll go peacefully when the cops get here."

"Not the cops, Walter. The board of directors."

"No!" screamed Walter in sudden terror. "Anything but that! Police brutality, the gas chamber at Folsom—but not the board!" He began dragging himself desperately toward the elevator, but it seemed to be a couple of miles away. Then its doors slid open, revealing a lone figure.

"Holy mackerel!" said Joe Pete.

Promptly at 8:00 the next morning, just off LouLor Airlines Flight 17, old Norton, young Norton, Keswick, Vladimir Arcati, and Benny Blochkopf, a ninety-year-old risk-capital philanthropist who also sat on the boards of several Arcati-run dummy corporations and diploma mills in the Lesser Antilles, all filed into Walter Neff's hospital room. Office wags would later call them "the Bedpan Board."

Keyes made his presentation. Then young Norton lounged back insultingly in his chair, sneered like a basilisk, and said, "So Neff snuck into your precious office after hours and used some sacrosanct dictating machine. Big deal. Shall we also reprimand every employee who tucks a few paper clips into her brassiere before going home?"

"Reprimand . . ." murmured Walter in a pained voice. "No, please—this would destroy my mother if she found out."

"Reprimand?" said Keyes. "Walter, you had a neurotic need

to betray the parent company and my love and trust. It would be masochistic of me to play father figure after that. No, Walter, you're the D.A.'s baby boy now. You've confessed to cold-blooded felonious homicide with malice aforethought, conspiracy to defraud, destroying evidence, harboring an accomplice, obstruction of justice—and that could be just the tip of the iceberg."

"No, no," said Walter, "I swear to you, that is all there is."

Blochkopf was sobbing uncontrollably. "What are you, Keyes, a butcher? The man lies before us on a sickbed! He's one of us! You don't rat on one of your own! The police have no right to pry into our affairs!"

"In point of fact," said the urbane Arcati reasonably, "this is not a criminal matter—it is a medical matter. Walter Neff is a victim of a physical malaise caused by unfavorable surroundings. Air pollution and so forth. I used to see many such cases in the Congo—a white man is driven wild by the jungle heat, he sweats, he develops a high fever, he kills. *Hélas!* In the tropics, we treat such a man with quinine."

"Besides," said old Norton, "another thing in Walter's favor is that he's no habitual criminal. He's no penny-ante sneak dipping into the till for years and years, the way your father did, Keyes, I might add. Walter thinks big. He bided his time and he went for the big score."

"Yeah, Keyes," said Walter. "You know me. I wanted to hit it for the limit."

"Keyes," continued old Norton, "your petty nose-to-the-grindstone habits have their place. But General Fidelity also needs men who can grasp the big picture. Like Walter. Executive material. And you want him locked up?"

"Police!" sobbed Blochkopf. "A tragedy!"

"Still," said Arcati smoothly, "there may be a moral solution to this snag. Let's say we fire him. Then we're in a position to give him his own company. I have a slush fund in Brazil that needs a chief executive officer—"

"What about my pension plan?" cried Walter in outrage.

Young Norton lolled arrogantly with his feet on the bed, as if to remind Keyes of the shoeshine days in Cambridge. "The police, the D.A.—simply fools. Beneath our notice. But what if that TV sob sister from *Wall Street Week* gets wind of this? Our stock would go through the floor."

"I don't care if our stock poisons every man, woman, and child who touches it!" shrieked Blochkopf. "No cops!"

"There's no need for hysterics, Keyes," continued young Norton. "But you *want* a crisis, don't you? You hold thirty percent of the stock—maybe you want to force us all out, so you can have star billing."

Keswick, the corporation counsel, spoke up. "Murder is technically a legal violation, Mr. Norton. Mr. Neff *is* in an embarrassing position. Perhaps a sabbatical—"

"Please!" cried Walter, writhing in torture. "Turn me over to the D.A. bound and gagged, hang me right here on the spot— but not a sabbatical!"

"Walter didn't murder anybody!" screamed Blochkopf. "*Keyes* did it! I saw him!" Tears of compassion dribbled from the corners of his mouth.

"Time for a vote," said old Norton. Keyes, not being a board member, went into the hall. A few minutes later, Keswick came out and sullenly slunk onto the elevator.

When Keyes was called back in, he learned that all but Keswick had voted to keep the matter confidential, on one firm condition: that Walter agree to accept medical treatment for his gunshot wounds.

Young Norton licked his lips contemptuously and said, "We also voted to fire Keswick from the board. I nominated his replacement."

Keyes knew that the choice had been calculated to humiliate him. He smiled ironically. "Who is he? Joe Pete?"

"It's a *she!*" yelled Blochkopf in triumph. "A noble grief-stricken widow. A respected member of the community. She used to be a nurse. She can be a consultant on medical insurance. And as pretty as Barbara Stanwyck!"

The board had unanimously elected Phyllis Dietrichson.

- Barton Keyes went back to his routine at General Fidelity, but his heart wasn't in it, and at the end of 1977 he sold his stock and retired to Key Largo.
- Old Norton died in 1978, and young Norton sold General Fidelity to the Dr Pepper Company. The stock split six for one.
- Joe Pete embezzled $275 from General-Pepper, and was put out to pasture with a $750,000-a-year deal as a consultant for the purchase of janitorial supplies.
- Nettie, wooed by a head hunter specializing in discreet executive secretaries, took a job with a wealthy private employer at San Clemente.
- Benny Blochkopf inadvertently swallowed some of his own saliva and died of a toxic reaction.
- Keswick is unemployed.
- Shapiro became chief counsel for a California safari park.
- Vladimir Arcati now manages a prestigious money-market fund.
- Roy Neary and the electric-power company he worked for were prosecuted for fraudulent collusion. They had used public monies and electrical equipment to fake a series of UFO visitations, including that of a gigantic "mother ship," to collect insurance for malfunctioning company vehicles and local power failures. Neary would shortly jump bail and perpetrate the same hoax in Indiana. But his

conviction in California remained the final bitter triumph of Keyes' belief that wherever there's a thrill, there's a swindle.

- Walter Neff took a medical leave to recuperate, accompanying Phyllis Dietrichson on a Caribbean cruise. On October 12, 1977, Walter and Phyllis vanished from shipboard and were never seen again. On August 4, 1978, exactly one year from the day Nettie discovered the first confession, Keyes, enjoying sashimi at La Japonais restaurant in Key Largo, bit into a morsel of shark meat containing an ankle bracelet engraved "Phyllis." He almost choked on it.

Now at West Egg

Once I wrote down on the empty spaces of a time-
table the names of those who came to Gatsby's
house that summer. It is an old time-table now,
disintegrating at its folds.... But I can still
read the gray names.
—*The Great Gatsby,* by F. Scott Fitzgerald

From the Diners Club International, then, came John Citizen and George T. Worthington and J. N. Travers, and Judith Shaw the account executive and her associate Robert Marston, who had the Diners Doublecards, and Jeffrey Rice and his sales manager, Cato Johnson, who also had the Doublecards until they lost them last summer up in Maine. And Macy Shopper, and John Q. Traveler (with a steamer trunk forwarded by Assist-Card International), and John Q. Customer, from 456 Main Street, Anytown, New York, who stood in a corner and showed his Irving Trust checkbook to whosoever came near, and John Q. Public, whose Korvettes charge plate, they say, turned to dust one winter afternoon for no good reason at all.

John Doe came from 1234 Main Street, Hometown, U.S.A., as I remember from his mail-order luggage tag, but once he got drunk and produced a Saks Fifth Avenue charge plate that said he was from 150 Elm Street, Anywhere, U.S.A., and when I knew him at the Hertz No. 1 Club he lived at 123 Main Street, City and State.

Of American Express cardholders there were C. F. Frost, and Jacques LeGrand, reputed to be French, and from England Charles F. Frost. Also from England were J. S. Smith (the son) with his Habitat card, and John Williams, with Access, and H. Stephens, who carried Barclaycard, and Rodney Cake, of Mill House, Nightingale Road, Horsham, Sussex, whose solid-gold business card was said to have cleaned him out at two hundred and twenty-six pounds, and who killed himself by putting his right hand in a cash machine. James P. ("Jim") Hayden came there, too, for he had Carte Blanche, and so did Clark Grimes and J. A. Modern, and Modern's girls.

R. A. Hoover was there with Wings, his Eastern Airlines personal credit card, three days before it was declared void. He arrived always with two Bankcard holders. They were never quite the same ones, but they were so like one another that it inevitably seemed they were cousins to the great American families listed in the telephone directory. I have forgotten their names—J., I think, or else L., and their last names were always Rogers or Harris.

In addition to all these, I can remember that Barbara S. Gottlieb, who was well over sixty, was there at least once—she had a Social Security card—and Carl Rhodes, with Blue Cross coverage, dead now, and John Parker, the Brooklyn Savings Bank Money Check customer who not long afterward strangled a teller, and Visa's young F. W. Weeks, who had his credit cut off in the war.

A man who claimed that his middle name had been Integrity since 1892 came there often, and so did Specimen Signature, whom we called by some other name that, if I ever knew it, I have forgotten.

All these people came to Gatsby's house in the summer, and all of them were turned away.

Supreme Court Roundup

WASHINGTON, May 8—*The Supreme Court took the following actions today:*

FIRST AMENDMENT

In a landmark decision, the Court ruled unanimously in favor of a twelve-year-old plaintiff who sought damages on account of being denied the chance to audition for the Clint Eastwood role in the motion picture *Maddened Rustlers*. The Court's opinion, written by Chief Justice Happ, argued that exclusion of the little girl was "tactless." The case was not decided, as had been expected, on the ground of sex discrimination; rather, the Justices invoked the First Amendment's guarantee of freedom of expression. The Court thus affirmed for the first time the constitutional right to a screen test.

SEARCH AND SEIZURE

Overturning the "dog's breakfast" doctrine of search and seizure, the Court held unconstitutional the Drug Enforcement Administration's system of obtaining search warrants, under which a judge who issues a warrant receives a warm, wet kiss on the mouth, while a judge who refuses a warrant is reclassified as a Controlled Substance. Justice Happsberger, writing for the majority, said that such procedures "lean upon the delicately coiffed maiden of the Fourth Amendment with the great ugly brutish heavily muscled shoulder of procedural error," and cited Judge Cheerful Hand's famous dictum "I shall keep at it with these metaphors till I'm old and it's unbecoming."

TAXES

Without hearing arguments on the issue, the Court ordered the Internal Revenue Service to desist at once from collecting personal income taxes—a practice that Justice Hapenny defined in his opinion as "a crying shame" and "the product of diseased minds." He pointed out that the government could easily collect the same amount of money by manufacturing and selling wall plaques that say "UNCLE SAM LOVES YOUR FIRST NAME HERE."

CONTROVERSY

In one of their occasional "piggyback" decisions, the Justices resolved some of the long-standing issues that clog the Court calendar. They ruled that nurture is more influential than nature, that men make history, that Iago is driven by motiveless malignancy, that one isn't too many and a thousand is enough, that there is an earthly paradise, and that Don Bucknell's nephew Ed doesn't look anything like Richard Gere. Justice Hapworth dissented but was too polite to say so.

MORAL BLIGHT

Citing "want of attractiveness" as a reason, the Court declined, 7–2, to hear an appeal by the publisher of two so-called men's magazines, *Rude Practices* and *Men's Magazine.* In the majority opinion, Chief Justice Happ explained that appellant's arguments were "unprepossessing and—let's be frank about it—just incredibly disingenuous." Dissenting, Justices Happer and Happner said they wanted to pretend to hear the case and then "fix appellant's wagon" for "putting out such a typographically unappetizing publication."

In a related decision, the Justices unanimously refused to hear a song written by a Kleagle of the Ku Klux Klan.

CRIMINAL

By a 9–0 vote, the Court held unconstitutional a New York City statute that would have mandated criminal convictions for suspects who fail to take policemen aside and "read them their duties." The statute had required that suspects deliver these "Caliban warnings" to policemen in order to remind them of their power of life and death, their obligation to attend to personal hygiene, etc. The Court, in an opinion by Justice Happell, contended, "Who can doubt that this would be the first step toward compelling suspects to serve their arresting officers creamed chicken on toast points?"

GIBBERISH

The Court voted unanimously not to review a case in which a court of appeals struck down a lower federal court's decision to vacate an even lower court's refusal to uphold a ruling that it is not unconstitutional to practice "reverse discrimination." Chief Justice Happ, who wrote the opinion, said that the Court "is not, nor will it consent to be, a body of foolosophers easily drawn into jive baloney-shooting." The Modern Language Association filed a brief of *amicus curiae* ("friendly curiosity").

GREED

Splitting 8–1, the Court upheld the constitutionality of a federal program for the redistribution of wealth. Under the program, which is known as "horizontal divestiture," rich people are asked to lie down, and poor people then divest them of their money. Justice Happold, dissenting, said that the program would diminish the impact of a standing Court order requiring that income in excess of $15,000 a year be bused across state lines to achieve bank-account balances.

As is their custom, the Justices closed the session with an informal musicale, playing a Corelli *gigg*. Justices Hapgood, Hapworth, Happner, and Happer performed on violin, Justice Happell on bassoon, Justice Happsberger on harpsichord, Justice Happold on oboe, Justice Hapenny on flute, and Chief Justice Happ on viola d'amore.

Lobster Night

Earl took me to the Café Chromosome. His choice, my birth-day, his money, party of two. The effects there are very effec-tual: the famous Shivering Chandelier, six tables, twelve gold service plates engraved "Most People Are Not Here," seating capacity held artificially low so that the maximum number of the reservationless are turned away. I wanted to lower myself to the atmosphere. Stan and Florine came in. Earl said to me, "Are you sure that Stan is as faithful to you as he makes out? Because he told me a different story." I hated Earl then for his talebearing and could think of but one thing—twosomes—and could do but two things—go, and send Stan a note to say I would be at the place next door. My choice, my birthday, my money, party of one.

When I got to Chez les Cent Un Dalmatiens, Earl was there, flecked with impatience, and when he said we must talk, I shook my head no: there was just enough darkness for blurting and just enough light for embarrassment, just enough privacy for a regrettable scene and just enough exposure for a classic scene, just enough food in the kitchen to turn Earl rather ami-able and just enough drink in the cellar to turn him perfect; but when he tried to go, I couldn't bear to be without someone to be with—not, at least, while Stan and Florine were forking it in next door, Stan longing for my next message, which said, "No. Not her. *Me.*" Which I was too proud to send, so I suggested we share a cab to another place.

At Lord Lipid's, men in livery kowtowed, and the drinks came in cups of bridle leather. Earl asked me what I wanted, and I said Stan, but Earl said that wasn't what he meant. "Then," I said coldly, "I want to have my signature honored. I want to be swathed in miles of challis." Earl looked hurt. A combo played, hautboy and cocktail comb. I had tears in my eyes, I had hurt him, I wanted to have had a convalescent brother kiss me through the dining-room window at Field Place. Stan came in. He could only stay a moment, Florine waited. He asked me why I was upset, and I said because I didn't mind his having dinner with Florine. He said they were having drinks, not dinner, and in any case didn't I know how very, very pretty I was even though what I had said was the sheerest nonsense? A wrong and senseless joy—but at that Earl picked up the bread knife and held it to the throat of a loaf of bread, saying, "Don't worry—you two are next." Then he dropped the knife and looked hurt. Stan said, "A little lithium would do no harm there," and went away—he missed Florine, who was outside and was also very pretty.

To cheer Earl up, I took him in a cab to Early Bacon, where they have bunny china. He was so hurt that I wanted to live with him to a ripe grandevity. I held his hand for a second. Then Florine arrived. Washed-out, I thought, as pretty women so often get; but when at the door they made her put on a plastic bib although she insisted she couldn't eat, to see her humiliated made me feel more kindly. She told us she had meant to live with Earl but that Stan had said couples need companionship and had moved in on her. I watched Earl swallow this. I flirted with her, wanting only to hurt Stan, Earl, and her. Then, knowing I must leave the pair of them to reconcile, I went out and hailed a taxi.

At the Horse Leech Pub, the wooden tables had new varnish over initials in old varnish, some of them carved with my own utility blade. I brooded about the past, I wanted to settle hash. Stan came in and said, "Nothing can be done. And when I say nothing, I mean there are certain things we could try that would be pointless."

"Such as?"

To my left, a man half turned away from a woman was saying, "It's really wonderful how everything's gone just right for me." I wanted to paste him one, but first I wanted to know too much luxury.

Stan said, "It would be pointless for you and me to get it on again. And when I say pointless, I mean it would be wonderful."

I refused. I wanted him to say of me, "I love her, although there's no denying that she's headstrong." I rose to leave, but he said he could force me to pack a vanity case and join him at his hideaway on Briar Island. I tried to make him go back to Florine, but he wouldn't, saying she was quite a woman and he planned to write her biography—a thing, I believe, few men would have bothered to do. I wanted no one to write of me, "She couldn't want it for herself."

En route to the Island, we took a taxi to Say Say and crouched on our old mat under the trellis in the tatami room. I felt guilty about betraying Earl, but there, in Stan's presence, I saw infidelity to be the act that makes fidelity possible for others. As it turned out, for complicated reasons we never went to Briar Island at all. Earl and Florine sent a message by cab announcing that they were coming over in a taxi. Stan wanted to hang around, but I said what if Earl and Florine then showed up, confidently expecting us to have bolted? Stan wouldn't listen, and I felt deceived, though of course it wasn't my business to see that people weren't deceived. When Earl and Florine arrived, each with the other, I asked her to cab along with me to a place uptown.

The Grouse Box was charred black on the outside and blood-red inside, full of dates falling in love because they had been thrust from insupportable solitude into one of a few infrequent and eagerly anticipated evenings out. Florine went to the ladies', and when she came back, she said, "Don't look now. Pay phone on the wall. Heavyset guy talking on it, kneeling." I knew how she felt, for we had been in it together—the marches, taunts, hoarseness, purple banners: Had we done it just for this? I asked her what she wanted. "A fast waltz in a drawing room lighted by innumerable candles." I liked her honesty. We joked about Earl and Stan, how they had lately been wearing their pants very high to shorten the chest and make it look powerful, and she told me of items she had read in the *Newsletter of the Affairs of Others,* and I sensed that we could be lovers if one of us were a man with bedroom eyes.

Momentarily, Earl dashed in and said Stan was to follow in a taxi. The three of us had a painful interview, Earl demanding to know if Florine wished to renounce him for Stan or if I had enough money to bribe Stan to support me.

I would not answer.

Florine would. "Oh, you and your ultimata!"

"You call that a decision? Well. This is it, then."

"If this were *it,* it wouldn't be this," said Florine, and ran off.

Earl was too depressed to stay, so we left a note for Stan and took a cab to a place in the vicinity.

At Villa Alive, the menu listed only one dish, with the annotation "An Alternative." We had hardly touched the water course when Stan appeared in the doorway, saw us, and shot out. I asked Earl if he had noticed, but he wouldn't discuss it, and years later I heard that he still didn't speak of the matter. He told me he was fairly certain I owed him a commitment, since Florine had flat rejected him. I asked him what he wanted. "To break your legs if you're ever unfaithful to me." I wanted to dispute this modest view of love, but scarcely had I pronounced the opening lines of my argument—"This wickit ymaginacioun, quhich by his name is clepit Jelousye"—when I found myself in a taxi next to him.

At Other Fish to Fry, white tile set off the barflies, taproom boasts, trenchermen, and couples. In the booth behind me, voices:

"Their sole amandine sounds nice."

"I would quarrel with that, Valerie, I'm afraid. Though you are free to disagree. I'd like nothing more than to hear you disagree. Show some spine, Valerie, for a change."

"Well, to be honest—maybe I'm way out of line on this one, but I'm pretty positive that I probably don't want the sole, I almost think."

"Among aware, intelligent people there will always be some difference of opinion. You should have the sole, Valerie, even if it is the wrong choice. Nobody's keeping score."

"Well, your willingness to discuss this has meant a lot. I really appreciate it. I guess I'll just have the gravy."

I ordered sole amandine, Earl a house salad—snail shells and birds' nests in vinaigrette, which returned him to his theme. "Even some plants build nests, you know. Ever heard of the carpenter gardenia?"

"Not recently."

He took some color slides from his wallet and held them one at a time to the light in such a way that I couldn't help but view them. "Number One, the male gardenia painstakingly constructs a maisonette for its spouse. Yes, throughout the vegetable kingdom pairing is the rule. Number Two, a male and a female copperhead wend their way aboard the ark at Tallahassee's World of Couples. Number Three, these bug mates feel no need for speculation on the natural order as they are united in an informal mid-morning ceremony. Number Four, hmm, that one's a disappointment."

A dazzling offer—but I wanted room, rope, more room for my rope. Stan came in and told us he was terrified of keeping his promises to Florine. I thought of him all alone and Florine in God knows what kind of nickel-and-grab. I wanted to say "Go" and then have the prudence to say "Now come back." I got him outside but couldn't find him a taxi, so I helped him make his way, on foot, through a light drizzle, to a place.

At the Blue Pill, the room was warm and steamy, and I felt as if the world were enveloped in a vaporous envelope. I wanted Stan to suggest with his hand a place in the air, I wanted to let my weight take me up and into the place, to be caught and set down safely and left alone. We sat across from each other— between us a square of white tablecloth, a small volume of air. I wanted someone to force a spray of stephanotis into my arms, I wanted every seed pearl on the Eastern seaboard sewn to my bust.

"Do you know how fond I am of you all?" he said. "You and your sweet habit of shrinking and waffling at the slightest question, Florine and her sweet habit of repeating society news—how can I share what isn't mine?"

I was holding my breath.

"Earl and our common memory of service in the barbiturate wars—"

I wanted to say of him years afterward, "He was the only one who didn't try to railroad me into something terminal."

"You have your whole lives ahead of you."

At that point, Florine burst in. "Good heavens! What are you two doing here? Why aren't you confronting Earl and me at the In Luck Rice Corp. East?" She said she had to go back, but Stan suddenly drew on our sympathies with an imaginary ailment, so there was no question of her leaving. We ordered champagne and candy, and for Stan a cot. He sat under the covers, propped up with pillows, one hand tucked into Florine's placket and the other into mine. I wanted to know little of the area save for this rude map.

"It's tempting to ask one of you to marry me. But later I'd have to chuck her for the other one."

"Serial chucking."

"Maybe we're changing."

"Not again!"

We arranged to all four meet for a nightcap at a place we had heard of over in Jersey.

At Adjust Moon, there was no atmosphere, except for the Dribbling Shotglasses, with which we toasted my birthday. We all held hands across the paper tablecloth, pleased with one another, Florine and I much, much more comfortable together, until Earl spoiled things by writing on a matchbook the name of the person each of us would end up with and then, without showing it, burning it in the ashtray. At a time when so many might despair, we got out of hand. First Florine and I defied

Stan and Earl, then Stan and Florine defied Earl and me, we
defied them, Stan and I defied Florine and Earl, they defied us,
and finally Earl and Stan defied Florine and me. Everyone
refused to leave everyone. Luxurious lobster nights!—but Earl
said that we confused happiness with our private interests, that
instead we should confuse it with his and pair off arbitrarily in
the normal way, that the course of evolution could not be
changed by a foursome in a single nightclub. "Moon gas," said
Florine. Earl said that, granted, he didn't know which one he
wanted, her or me, but whichever it was, he wanted that one all
to himself, he wanted to reject the other one, he wanted to
cultivate hostility between the two of us. "Be fair," said Stan.
Earl said he didn't want fairness, he wanted me or her, though
naturally we were free to disagree. We did disagree. Earl said,
"I'll give you this: you might be on to something. But you're
going a dumb way with it."

   Goodbye, Earl, and good luck!

We didn't try enough, we didn't give him enough of a chance.
He didn't love us enough, not enough for my money, not
enough to go around. There wasn't enough love in him to dust
a fiddle. True enough. Well, why make a meal of it? Enough
said.

There were spots we hadn't hit yet, so the three of us hit them.
We went to the Kidney Garden, and the French Way, and
Unter dem Dirndl. Everybody was awake, the Garland restaurant grills were heated to a surface temperature impossible to
get on a home unit, people whose greed was different from ours
in some cases and in some cases not were ordering all the
courses in the correct progression and saying "What's the damage?" We went to Parolles', and Ovos Fervidos, and Three Ack
Emma. Customers gazed at the far rims of their cups and glasses

as they drank; we thought of Earl, of the loneliness between the time you abandon what wasn't enough and the time you find what won't be enough. We went to How's Your Father, to the Cod's Head Inn and the Cod's Head du Soir. There were many arrangements of people talking while someone present or absent got left out; alphabets of elbow positions on tables; waits, delicacies, tall orders. We crumpled our linen napkins, which opened again on their own, and then we went dancing to a combo—drum, vocalist, and another drum—at Necktie Party. At dawn, we walked, changing places: man woman woman, woman man woman, woman woman man. The streets were empty. We had no plan. At an intersection, a red van turned the corner toward us. A second, a third, a fleet followed. Their sides were painted with the words "Swinging and Revolving Doors—Sales—Service—Repair—Modernization." Then, as the first van passed us, it sounded its klaxon. Van after van caught the spirit. Horns filled the air in awkward greeting. We waved, and walked for a while longer, three abreast: Stan on the inside, lest slops hurled from a window soil Florine or me; Florine on the outside, lest a taxicab splatter me or Stan; me in the center, lest Stan or Florine feel left out.

Pepys's Secret Diaries!

Now the appearance of Hitler's diaries—genuine or not, it almost doesn't matter in the end—reminds us of the horrible reality. . . .
—*Newsweek,* May 2, 1983

IT BEGAN AS THE RESTORATION OF THE STUARTS . . .
AND ENDED IN A SHATTERING BLITZKRIEG!

Skulking back in the labyrinth of time to the libertine intrigues of the seventeenth century, an ardent freelance memorabilia hunter has tracked down an unsuspected cache of evidence that shrouds all previous historical forgeries in a new light. Diaries kept by Samuel Pepys, a key insider in the British Navy Office, were reportedly dispatched to Cambridge University after his death in 1703; but somewhere on the east herbaceous border of the campus, they were dispersed and lost in a wanton wheelbarrow crash. Not until two years ago did the anonymous source, pursuing leads obtained in bawdy badinage with an unidentified coterie, pick up the trail in the exclusive recesses of Magdalene College Library, Cambridge, where the sixty volumes had been cleverly hidden for centuries in ingeniously constructed glass display cases. The following excerpts, which have already sparked a blizzard of gossip, were decoded with the aid of the sophisticated Interpol Penmanship Squad from the cipher in which Pepys wrote on newly authenticated seventeenth-century legal pads.

[Jan.] 28th, [1661]
At the office all morning, thence to an ale-house to be re-

freshed. I did talk of nothing but Cromwell's body. The thought of this dead Puritan, with his unfortunate hair-cut, the worst thing that I ever saw, did vex me greatly. I warned him not to close the theatres; and to have some love affairs, as the German leaders do; but no. By and by he was therefore killed of natural causes; on whose orders, I confess, I know not. Dined; thence to the theatre to see a thing by Dryden, the author of *Brown-Shirts à la Mode; or, Scum and Bungl'rs,* wherein was the most pleasant speech. His new play did likewise make my heart rejoice; being called *Operation Seraglio,* with Nell [Gwyn] very pretty in Bavarian dress.

[Jan.] 29th, [1661]
Very well pleased with our Charles II, who ever is up to his old tricks with women. How lewdly did he talk, and with how much wit, when I arrived at White Hall with my secret directive for trading to the Germans, in exchange for the greatest fleet of ships that can be imagined, our blueprints for the invention of the proscenium stage! After dinner with my wife to see a play of Congreve's, *Lust for Power;* the world never can hope ever to see again so much wickedness so prettily done, or so well concluded.

[Sept.] 2d, [1666]
Up late last night, when there came a knock on the door telling us of a great fire raging in the city. Thence to the window, and thought the blaze to be in Drury Lane at the farthest. Having in an hour's time walked to that place, I did determine that it was only a lighting rehearsal for an amateur masque, *The Night of the Brok'n Glass;* yet elsewhere in the city was every body running this way and that. Lord! These hotheads! They live in a dream world. Hearing a fine thunder of poetic bombast, they would perceive the unimaginable sound of real Germans in the sky with muskets; a thought for which I pray God

forgive me; as, for aught I know, He did do; for on my way home, amidst the disorder, I spied the prettiest pair of knickers that ever was revealed to any man.

[Feb.] 2d, [1667]
To see Wycherley's new play, *The Smoothie Englishman;* the most cunning that I ever did see; mightily commended for its leading part, a Prime Minister who gives away of Czechoslovakia the most that ever I saw in my life, and thus loses his mistresses. I was sick to see it, but yet would not but have seen it; for this man Wycherley is indispensable to me, that I might the better draft my confidential guidelines for the behaviour of Government ministers in future.

[May] 31st, [1669]
Up very betimes, and had another meeting with the King at White Hall, on the Germans' insulting counter-offer of the rights to some boring, preachifying play-scripts about Teutonic mythological personages in exchange for a beach-head at Southampton. The King very angry, having lately seen so few people in the pit for Nell's performance as Lady Himmler in *The Unfathomable Penny-Pincher;* a travelling troupe of Russian mimes being said now-a-days to carry away all the people, as having more powerful players with the most luxuriant moustaches. The King did then speak of tough reprisals; but whatever comes of these, I must forbear to record; for thus ends the keeping of my Journal, I growing blind. And therefore, from this time forward, may the world know no more than it is fit for them to know, save this one final note:

Dined with my wife; thence to see Farquhar's new play, *The Jews' Stratagem; or Love Preserv'd:* the greatest and most artful thing that I could ever live to see; and so, we to a drinking-house, called The World's End: merry as I never saw it.